Works

ON EMERSON
AND OTHER ESSAYS

THE WORKS OF MAURICE MAETERLINCK

ESSAYS

PLAYS

POEMS

HOLIDAY EDITIONS

On Emerson
And Other Essays

BY
MAURICE MAETERLINCK

Translated by
MONTROSE J. MOSES

NEW YORK
DODD, MEAD AND COMPANY
1920

ENGLISH I

CONTENTS

ON EMERSON
AND OTHER ESSAYS

FOREWORD

THE three essays contained in this volume
have for the first time been brought together for English readers. The one on
Emerson has served its purpose as a
preface to seven essays of Emerson, translated by Mlle. Mali, who took the
pseudonym of I. Will. The other two
were originally intended and were used as
introductions to extensive selections made
and translated by M. Maeterlinck from the
works of Ruysbroeck and Novalis. In
amended form, the three essays may be
found in the French edition of "The
Treasure of the Humble."

At his simplest, it is not an easy matter
to translate Maeterlinck. Especially difficult
is it when one is dealing with a double
mystic, or rather with the mystic Maeter-

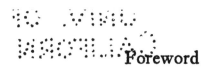

linck's interpretation of three transcendental thinkers. Many times has our
author expressed himself on the subject of
the translator's art, and it is well to remember these words of his relative to the problem confronting him when he attempted a
translation of "Macbeth":

"It is that secret life which it is important
to understand and to reproduce as well as
one can. Extreme prudence is required,
since the slightest false note, the smallest
error, may destroy the illusion and destroy
the beauty of the finest page."

But it is a question whether translation
means alone the understanding of the secret
life of the piece, or whether it does not also
mean faithfulness in reproducing, as near as
possible, the word-structure and the form.
For example, translating Maeterlinck's
translation of passages from Emerson, one
is forced to depart materially from the ex-

Foreword

act tenor of Emerson's thought, and to forsake the compact reticence of his style. And it is not far wrong to consider these quoted passages in the French as almost paraphrases. Yet the secret life of Emerson's philosophy is there, even though I have considered it best to quote Emerson exactly. And while reading Maeterlinck's essay on his avowed master and greatest influence, it will be noted how completely and how unconsciously Emerson's thoughts have been assimilated by Maeterlinck. In his essay there are many echoes of "The Over-Soul" and "Spiritual Laws."*

Maeterlinck's interest in the mediæval mystic, Ruysbroeck, must have begun while he was a student at the Jesuit College of Saint-Barbe. It was in 1891 that "The Ornament of Spiritual Marriages" was

---

*See Hamilton Osgood's "Maeterlinck and Emerson," *Arena*, 15 : 563-73, March, 1896; *Poet-Lore*, Jan.-Mar., 1898, 10 : 76-84.

Foreword

translated from the Flemish, while in 1895
there followed the equally difficult task of
translating from the German Novalis's
"The Disciples at Saïs" and "The Fragments." Only the year before, 1894,
Maeterlinck had prefaced Mlle. Mali's
volume. When it is recollected that 1889
saw the publication of "La Princesse Ma-
leine" and "Serres Chaudes," and that "Le
Tresor des Humbles" (1896) was his first
book of essays, one may readily understand
what an important part Ruysbroeck, Novalis, and Emerson had in the forming of
Maeterlinck's sympathy with such thought.
The philosophic studies that comprise the
following volume represent, therefore, the
sources of his philosophic inspiration.
Maeterlinck once showed to an American
acquaintance his much worn volume of
Emerson's "Essays," heavily underscored
and filled with marginal notes. This enthusiasm of the disciple is also discernible in

Foreword

his attitude toward Ruysbroeck and Novalis.

In his essay on the former there are many more original extracts given than in the other essays. And though one may not always agree with Maeterlinck as to the equal excellence of these passages, one can, nonetheless, be in hearty sympathy with the fervour which he displays and with the true conviction he expresses.

Maeterlinck's point of view as a biographer is likewise of significance. He deals in all three essays, with men to whom the external event was nought beside the inner life. Save in the instance of the pathetic love tragedy of Novalis, he does not relish fact as much as he does the discovery of the soul's expression. He hastens over the few events in Ruysbroeck's sainted life, relieved that he can pass quickly to the core of his philosophy. And as for Emerson, he altogether ignores locality and time. On reading the essay, one might as well be noting a disembodied spirit.

These essays, therefore, being very largely abstract, I have thought it best to give a close rendering, departing from the form only where more clearness might be gained.

In regard to Ruysbroeck, there are a few facts which might serve to heighten the account to be found in Maeterlinck's essay. Though the dates of his birth and death are given, it is well to realise that the old monk lived to the ripe age of one hundred and six years, and that, at the last, when it was heard how the Admirable John had passed away, there were many, so William Sharp records, who believed that Ruysbroeck had been the man nearest God since Christ. Throughout his life he exhibited unbounded spirituality, and claimed for himself that he never spoke unless within him he was moved by the Holy Ghost.

Foreword

His theology was thoroughly Catholic, and even as his expression of thought was mystical, so were his actions always attended by evidences of mystery. We are told by one of the monk's few English biographers, Dom Vincent Scully, C.R.L., who also wrote the article on Ruysbroeck in the "Catholic Encyclopedia," that "he loved to wander and meditate in the solitude of the forest adjoining the cloister; he was accustomed to carry a tablet with him, and on this to jot down his thoughts as he felt inspired so to do."

He was gentle and fond of life around him, even caring for the birds that came to be fed by him. So fervent was he that, like the Christus in the Passion Play, he oftentimes swooned while celebrating the Mass, through the sheer excess of his spiritual emotion. Legend has it that after his death, as he lay on his bier, there was performed a miracle, and that in his vestments he arose and celebrated for the last time the sacred mysteries of his beloved Church.

According to authorities, John Ruysbroeck, named after his town, in the same manner that Thomas à Kempis was named, was called by his contemporaries the Admirable Doctor and the Divine Doctor. For many years after his death his remains were most carefully preserved; but, in 1783, when Joseph II. suppressed Groenendael Priory, the relics were transferred to St. Gudule's, Brussels. There they remained until the French Revolution, during which upheaval they were lost.

The sainted Ruysbroeck was not officially recognised by his Church until within comparatively recent years. Many attempts were made to reward his virtues, but it was only by a decree dated December 1, 1908, that the title of "Blessed" was bestowed upon the devout mediæval monk.

Foreword

Though in 1869 a translation of Ruysbroeck was issued in France, done by Ernest Hello, himself a mystic and an influence on Maeterlinck, still to Maeterlinck belongs the credit of having given an impetus to recent French appreciation of Ruysbroeck. In England, portions of Maeterlinck's essay were published by Jane T. Stoddart in the London *Expositor* for 1894, and were amplified in a volume, "Ruysbroeck and the Mystics by Maurice Maeterlinck" (London, 1896). At a later date (London, 1905), Earle Baillie translated "Reflections from the Mirror of a Mystic" from Hello's "Œuvres Choisies de Rosbrock," with a few passages taken from the Latin text of Surius.

All commentators acknowledge with due gratefulness the work of Maeterlinck, though some Catholic scholars join in denying the statement made by him and others that Ruysbroeck was ignorant and only miraculously divined the science of his age and of the ages to come. Scully writes:

"A word of warning is needed against the assumption of some writers who would exalt the genius of Ruysbroeck by dwelling on what they term his illiteracy and ignorance. As a matter of fact, the works of the Blessed John manifest a mastery of the sacred sciences, and a considerable acquaintance even with the natural sciences of his day."

Add to this the enthusiasm of Surius, who is Ruysbroeck's true commentator, and whose admiration is reflected in Maeterlinck's own attitude:

"I do not believe that there is a man who can approach these magnificent and simple pages without great and singular profit. Let none excuse himself from reading this book on the plea of the inaccessible sublimity of

Foreword

Ruysbroeck. The great man has accustomed himself to all, and the most abandoned soul on earth may find again in reading him the path of salvation. Arrows dart from the pages of Ruysbroeck, aimed by no hand of man, but by the hand of God; and deeply they embued themselves in the soul of the reader who is a sinner. Innocent reader, reader of unstained robe, Ruysbroeck is at once most lowly and most sublime. In his description of the *Spiritual Espousals,* he surpasses admiration, he surpasses praise; all the commencement, all the progress, all the height, all the transcendent perfection of the spiritual life is there."

The reader of Maeterlinck's essay will infer that the Belgian has oftentimes been prompted to stretch his images to the very limits of consistency, in order to maintain the comparison of Ruysbroeck's style and manner with the foliage of Iceland or rather of the glacial regions. This license taken with the French language results in a tendency to coin words. Readers of Ibsen's "Brand" in the original soon recognise that the little Norwegian, in that respect, followed the custom of Carlyle. Yet Maeterlinck's enthusiastic approach cannot take from the fact that the quotations he makes from Ruysbroeck, while oftentimes rich in imagery and ardent in belief, are frequently illogical and prolix in construction—two faults often apparent in the untutored. Nevertheless, as a whole, the essay is of significance in the development of Maeterlinck, and his French is beautiful.

English readers can do no better than approach Novalis through the combined appreciations of Carlyle and Maeterlinck. Strange to say, the former adopts the same method adopted by the latter in his essay on Ruysbroeck. I mean, he includes in his

Foreword

text copious extracts from "The Fragments" of Novalis. And as examples of
mystic thought, we cull from the Carlyle
translations these excerpts:

"Philosophy is properly Home-sickness;
the wish to be everywhere at home."

"We are near awakening when we dream
that we dream."

"Man is the higher Sense of our Planet;
the star which connects it with the upper
world; the eye which it turns towards
Heaven."

"Life is a disease of the spirit; a work-
ing incited by Passion. Rest is peculiar to
the spirit."

"If our Bodily Life is a burning, our
Spiritual Life is a being burnt, a Combus-
tion (or, is precisely the inverse the case?);
Death, therefore, perhaps a Change of
Capacity."

Foreword

"There is but one Temple in the World; and that is the Body of Man. Nothing is holier than this high form. Bending before men is a reverence done to this Revelation in the Flesh. We touch Heaven, when we lay our hands on a human body."

"Man consists in Truth. If he exposes Truth, he exposes himself. If he betrays Truth, he betrays himself. We speak not here of Lies, but of acting against Conviction."

"The true Poet is all-knowing; he is an actual world in miniature."

"Goethe is an altogether practical Poet. He is in his works what the English are in their wares: highly simple, neat, convenient and durable. He has done in German Literature what Wedgewood did in English manufacture. He has, like the English, a natural turn for Economy, and a noble Taste acquired by Understanding. Both

Foreword

these are very compatible, and have a near affinity in the chemical sense . . . . 'Wilhelm Meister's Apprenticeship' may be called throughout prosaic and modern. The romantic sinks to ruin, the Poesy of Nature, the Wonderful. The book treats merely of common worldly things: Nature and Mysticism are altogether forgotten. It is a poetised civic and household History; the Marvellous is expressly treated therein as imagination and enthusiasm. Artistic Atheism is the spirit of the Book. . . . It is properly a *Candide*, directed against Poetry: the Book is highly unpoetical in respect of spirit, poetical as the dress and body of it are. . . . The introduction of Shakespeare has almost a tragic effect. The hero retards the triumph of the Gospel of Economy; and economical Nature is finally the true and only remaining one."

In the course of his essay, Maeterlinck

Foreword

has occasion to refer to Carlyle's attitude toward Novalis's second romantic attachment. In view of the profound effect of the child, Sophie, upon his work, many authorities offer varied excuses for his sudden change of heart, after the girl's death. Carlyle thus views the matter:

"Yet, perhaps, after all, it is only in a Minerva-Press Novel, or to the more tender Imagination, that such a proceeding would seem very blamable. Constancy, in its true sense, may be called the root of all excellence; and especially excellence is constancy in active well-doing, in friendly helpfulness to those that love us, and to those that hate us; but constancy in passive suffering, again, in spite of the high value put upon it in Circulating Libraries, is a distinctly inferior virtue, rather an accident than a virtue, and at all events is of extreme rarity in this world. To Novalis, his Sophie might still

Foreword

be a saintly presence, mournful and unspeakably mild, to be worshipped in the inmost shrine of his memory: but worship of
this sort is not man's sole business; neither
should we censure Novalis that he dries his
tears, and once more looks abroad with
hope on the earth, which is still, as it was
before, the strangest complex of mystery
and light, of joy as well as sorrow. 'Life
belongs to the living; and he that lives
must be prepared for vicissitudes.' The
questionable circumstance with Novalis
is his perhaps too great rapidity in
that second courtship; a fault or misfortune the more to be regretted, as this
marriage also was to remain a project, and
only the anticipation of it to be enjoyed by
him."

The German reader of Novalis will find
a copious bibliography extant. His chiefest
work, "Henry of Ofterdinger," has been

translated several times into English. (J. Owen, 1842, Cambridge, Mass.; H. H. Moore, 1853.)

Now, from these essays, which in their composition are contemporaneous with the practice of his art theories as exemplified in the marionnette dramas, Maeterlinck very well shows his tendency toward the essence, toward the spirit of things, so marked in his prose work of later years. There may be nothing new in his critical approach; there is certainly nothing controversial or scholastic in his biographical researches. But we note in these essays just that tendency in thought and in interest which was soon to find expression in "The Treasure of the Humble" and "Wisdom and Destiny."

And what may be said of Maeterlinck's theory of dramatic art is likewise true of his philosophic expression—for his attitude toward the theatre is an attitude toward life. He is an iconoclast in both respects,

which, I take it, means that he has redis-
covered for men the value of unseen forces.
Herein he declares his kinship with Emerson. His genius is no more tangible than
the genius of those he discusses. On the surface he is not more original than many another possessing a similar romantic style. In
his philosophy he has these three masters,
Ruysbroeck, Novalis, and Emerson; in his
poetry he is indebted to Poe, Whitman, and
Villiers de l'Isle-Adam—a queer group in
themselves. Though he has had to modify
his theory of drama, still his art theory is
his approach toward life, and this is his
great claim to originality.

He has utilised unseen forces; he regards
men simply as products of these forces. He
has made us feel the hidden powers that
mould us. He is more aloof than near, and
in this respect he is like Ruysbroeck and
Novalis. Not one of them has the democ-
racy of Emerson. But his artistic ability, so

Foreword

closely identified with his philosophic belief, which he always discourses upon with enthusiasm, is the new element which Maeterlinck has individualised. If there are those who believe that he has not received justification for his stand in modern thought, it might be well for them to compare some of the thoughts of Maeterlinck, herein expressed, with the philosophy of Henri Bergson.

In the preparation of this translation I have been in constant touch with those who are in sympathy with Maeterlinck and with mystic philosophy. To Professor Charles Downer, to the Reverend B. Stuart Chambers, and to others I am indebted for kind assistance and helpful suggestions. It is with pleasure that I acknowledge the courtesy of Mr. Alexander Teixeira de Mattos, who has kindly consented, with the permission of M. Maeterlinck, to allow the present translation. Mr. Teixeira is the

Foreword

official translator of Maeterlinck's works. The following editions were used:

L'Ornement des Noces Spirituelles, de Ruysbroeck l'Admirable, Traduit du Flamand et accompagné d'une Introduction par Maurice Maeterlinck. Bruxelles: Paul Lacomblez, 1910.

Les Disciples à Saïs et Les Fragments de Novalis, Traduits de l'Allemand et précédés d'une Introduction par Maurice Maeterlinck. Bruxelles: Paul Lacomblez, 1909.

Sept Essais d'Emerson: Confiance en Soi-même,—Compensation,—Lois de l'Esprit,—Le Poète,—Caractère,—L'Ame Suprême,—Fatalité. Traduits par I. Will (M. Mali), avec préface de Maurice Maeterlinck. Bruxelles: Paul Lacomblez, 1911.

MONTROSE J. MOSES.

New York, June, 1912.

EMERSON

"ONLY one thing matters," says Novalis, "and that is the search for our transcendental self." This self we discern at moments in the words of God, of poets, and of sages; in the depths of certain joys and sorrows; in sleep, in love and sickness, and in unforeseen crises where it signals us from afar, and points out our relations with the universe. Some philosophers devote themselves solely to this investigation, and they write those books in which only the extraordinary prevails. "What is there of value in books," says our author, "if it be not the transcendental and the extraordinary?" These philosophers are as painters striving to seize a likeness in the dark. Some trace abstract images for us, very remarkable but almost indistinct. There

31

are others who succeed in fixing an attitude
or an habitual gesture of the superior life.
A number exist who imagine strange beings. There are not many of these images. They are never alike. Some of them
are very beautiful, and those who have not
seen them dwell all their lives through like
unto men who have never come forth into
broad daylight. The lines of these images
are purer than the lines of heaven; but then
these figures appear to us so very distant
that we know not if they be alive, or if they
were created in our mind's eye. They are
the work of pure mystics, and man does not
as yet recognise himself in them. Others
there are whom we call poets, and who
speak to us indirectly of these things. A
third class of thinkers, elevating by one degree the myth of the old centaurs, has given
us an image of this occult identity more easy
of access—by blending the characteristics of
our apparent self with those of our superior

self. The countenance of our divine soul
smiles at times over the shoulder of the human soul, her sister, bent to the humble
labours of thought; and this smile, which
gives us a fleeting glimpse of all that lies
beyond thought, alone matters in the works
of men. . . .

There are not many who have shown us
that man is greater and more profound
than man, and who have thus succeeded in
fixing some few of the eternal allusions
which we encounter at every instant of life,
in a gesture, a sign, a look, a word,—in
silence and in the events which surround us.
The science of human greatness is the
strangest of sciences. None among us is
ignorant of it; but most of us do not know
that we possess it. The child that meets me
will not be able to tell his mother what he
has seen; however, as soon as his eyes have
sensed my presence, he knows all that I am,
all that I have been, all that I shall be, even

as well as my brother, and thrice better than myself. He knows me immediately in the past and in the future, in this world here, and in the other worlds, and, in turn, his eyes reveal to me the rôle I assume in the universe and in eternity.

Our infallible souls discern each other, and as soon as the child's glance has met mine,—my face, my attitude and the infinite which surrounds them and of which they are the interpreters,—he knows what to cling to; and though he cannot as yet distinguish the crown of an emperor from the wallet of a beggar, he has known me for one instant as exactly as God knows me.

It is true that we already act like gods, and our entire life passes amidst certitudes and infinite infallibilities. But we are blind men who play with precious stones along the roadway; and that man who knocks at my door expends, at the very moment he greets me, as many marvellous spiritual

treasures as the prince whom I have wrested
from death. I open to him, and in an instant he sees at his feet, as though from the
height of a tower, all that takes place between two souls. I judge the country woman
of whom I ask the way as profoundly as
though I had asked of her the life of my
mother, and her soul has spoken to me as
intimately as that of my betrothed. She
rises rapidly to the very greatest mysteries
before answering me; then she tells me
quietly, knowing on a sudden what I am,
that it will be necessary for me to take the
foot-path to the left for the village. If I
pass an hour amidst a crowd, without saying anything and without giving it a single
thought, I have judged a thousand times
the living and the dead. And which of
these judgments will be altered on the last
day? There are in this room some five or
six beings who speak of rain and of pleasant
weather; but above this miserable conversa-

really!? ✓ tion, six souls carry on a conversation which no human wisdom could approach without danger. And though they speak through their glances, their hands, their faces, and their assembled presence, they shall ever be ignorant of what they have said. However, they must wait the end of their elusive converse, and that is why they have an undefinable mysterious joy in their *ennui,* with out knowing what hearkens within them to all the laws of life, of death, of love,—laws which pass like inexhaustible rivers around the house.

Thus is it everywhere and always. We live only by virtue of our transcendental being, whose actions and thoughts momentarily pierce the envelope which surrounds us. I go to-day to see a friend whom I have never seen before, but I know his work, and I know that his soul is extraordinary, and that he has passed his life expressing it as exactly as possible, and in ac-

cordance with the duty of superior intel-
lects. I am full of uncertainty, and it is a
solemn hour. He enters, and at the opening of the door which reveals his presence,
every explanation of himself that he has
given us during a number of years falls
into dust. He is not what he believes himself to be. He is of another nature than his
thoughts. Once more we prove that the
emissaries of the spirit are ever faithless.
He has said many profound things of his
soul; but in that small time which divides
a glance that pauses from a glance that van-
ishes, I have learned all that he could never
say, and all that he was never able to cul-
tivate in his spirit. Henceforward, he belongs to me forever. Formerly we were
united by thought. To-day, something a
myriad times more mysterious than thought
gives us to each other. For years and years
we had waited this moment; and, behold,
we feel that all is useless, and, for fear of

silence, we, who were prepared to show each other secret and amazing treasures, talk about the time of day or about the setting sun, so as to give our souls an opportunity to wonder at each other and to bind themselves in another silence which the murmur of lips and of thought will not be able to disturb. . . .

In reality, we live only from soul to soul, and we are gods who do not know each other. If it is impossible for me this evening to bear my solitude, and if I should go among men, they will only tell me that the storm has beaten down their pears or that the late frost has closed the port. Is it for this that I have come? And yet, I shall soon go away from it, my soul as satisfied and as full of new richness and power as though I had passed these hours with Plato, Socrates, and Marcus Aurelius. What their mouth utters signifies nought besides what their presence declares, and it is impossible for man not to be great and admirable. What the mind thinks is of no importance beside the truth that we are,—a truth which silently affirms itself; and if, after fifty years of solitude, Epictetus, Goethe, and St. Paul should come to my island, they could tell me only what the smallest cabin-boy on their ship would say to me at the same time, and perhaps more directly.

In truth, what is strangest about man are his gravity and his hidden wisdom. The most frivolous amongst us never really laughs, and in spite of his efforts, never succeeds in losing a minute, for the human soul is attentive and does nothing useless. *Ernst ist das Leben:* Life is grave, and in the depths of our being, our soul has not yet smiled. On the other side of our involuntary emotions, we lead a marvellous life, still, very pure, and very certain, to which our hands which are outstretched, our eyes which are opened, and our unexpected

glances which meet, make continual allu-
sion. All our organs are the mystical ac-
complices of 'a superior being; and it is
never a man,—but a soul that we have
known. I did not see that poor wretch who
begged for alms on the steps before my
door. But I perceived some other thing: in
our eyes two identical destinies saluted each
other and loved each other, and, just when
he stretched forth his hand, the small door
of the house opened for an instant upon the
sea.

"In my dealing with my child," writes
Emerson [in "Over-Soul"], "my Latin and
Greek, my accomplishments and my money
stead me nothing. They are all lost on him;
but as much soul as I have avails. If I am
merely wilful, he gives me a Rowland for
an Oliver, sets his will against mine, one for
one, and leaves me, if I please, the degrada-
tion of beating him by my superiority of

strength. But if I renounce my will, and act for the soul, setting that up as umpire between us two, out of his young eyes looks the same soul; he reveres and loves with me."

But if it be true that the least amongst us is not able to make the slightest gesture without reckoning with the soul and with the spiritual kingdoms wherein the soul reigns, it is also true that the wisest scarcely ever thinks of the infinite which is moved by the opening of an eyelid, by the bending of the head, and by the closing of a hand. We live so far from ourselves that we are ignorant of nearly everything that occurs at the horizon of our being. We wander at random in the valley, without suspecting that all our actions are reproduced and gain their significance on the mountain top, and it is necessary at times for some one to come to us and say: Raise your eyes, see what you are, see what you do; it is not here that we live; it is up yonder, high above us, that we are. This glance exchanged in the dark; these words which had no meaning at the foot of the mountain—see what they become and what they signify further on the snowy summits; and how our hands, which we believe so feeble and so small, unknowingly reach God every moment.

Some there are who have come to us, and who have touched us in this manner on the shoulder, revealing to us yonder what takes place upon the glaciers of mystery. They are not many. There are three or four in this century! There were five or six in centuries past! And all that they have been able to say to us is nought in comparison with what has taken place and with that of which our soul is not ignorant. But what does it matter! Are we not like unto a man who has lost his eyesight during the first

years of his childhood? He has seen the
endless spectacle of beings. He has noted
the sun, the sea, and the forest. Now, and
always, these marvels are ever-present in his
make-up; and should you speak of them,
what will you be able to say to him, and.
what will your poor words be beside the
glade, the tempest, and the dawn which
still live in the depths of his spirit, and are
made part of his flesh? He will listen to
you, however, with an intense and astonished joy, and though he know all, and
though your words represent what he
knows more imperfectly than a glass of
water represents a broad river,—the small,
ineffective phrases which fall from the lips
of man will illumine for a moment the
ocean, and the light and shadow which
dwell amidst the darkness beneath his dead
lids.

The faces of this "transcendental me," of
which Novalis speaks, are probably innu-

merable, and not one of the mystic moralists has succeeded in studying the same.
Swedenborg, Pascal, Novalis, Hello, and
several others examine our relations with an
abstract, subtle, and very remote infinite.
They lead us upon mountains whose summits do not seem natural or habitable to us,
and where we often breathe with difficulty.
Goethe accompanies our soul upon the
shores of the sea of Serenity. Marcus
Aurelius places our soul on the hill-side of
an ideal humanity, its perfect excellence
somewhat tiresome, and beneath too heavy
a foliage of hopeless resignation. Carlyle,
the spiritual brother of Emerson, who in
this century has given us warning from the
other end of the valley, has brought before us in lightning strokes, upon a background of shadow and storm, of an unknown, relentlessly strange, the only
heroic moments of our being. He leads us
like a flock frightened by the tempest,

44

toward unknown and sulphurous pastures.
He drives us into the profoundest depths of
darkness, which he has discovered with joy,
and where shines alone the intermittent and
passionate star of heroes, and there he
abandons us, with a mischievous laugh, to
the vast reprisals of mysteries.

But at the same time, behold Emerson,
the good morning shepherd of pale
meadows, green with a new optimism, both
natural and plausible. He does not lead us
to the edge of a precipice. He does not
make us go from the humble and familiar
close, because the glacier, the sea, the
eternal snows, the palace, the stable, the
cheerless hearth of the poor, and the cot
of the sick,—all are found beneath the
same heaven, purified by the same stars, and
subjected to the same infinite powers.

He came for many just when he should
have come, and just when they had extreme
need of new explanations. Heroic hours

are less apparent, those of abnegation have not yet returned; there remains to us only our daily life; and even then we are not able to live without greatness. He has given an almost acceptable meaning to this life which no longer has its traditional horizons, and perhaps he has been able to show us that it is strange enough, profound enough, and great enough to have need of no other end than itself. He has no more knowledge of it than the others, but he affirms with more courage, and he has confidence in mystery. You must live—all of you who pass through days and years, without actions, without thoughts, without light, because, in spite of everything, your life is incomprehensible. You must live because no one has the right to avoid spiritual events in commonplace weeks. You must live because there are no hours without innermost miracles and without ineffable significance. You must live because there is

not an act, there is not a word, there is not
a gesture which escapes inexplicable claims
in a world "where there are many things to
do and few things to know."

There is neither a great nor a small life,
and a deed of Regulus or Leonidas has no
significance when I compare it with a moment of my soul's secret life. They might
have done what they did, or they might
not have done it—these things do not
touch the soul; and the soul of Regulus,
while he was returning to Carthage, was
probably as absorbed and as indifferent as
that of the mechanic going toward the fac-
tory. The soul is far removed from all our
deeds; it is too far from all our thoughts.
Deep within us it lives alone a life of which
it does not speak; and on the heights where
it exists, variety of being is no longer dis-
cerned. We move, weighted down beneath
the burdens of our soul, and there is no
symmetry between it and us. It probably

never thinks deeply of what we do, and this can itself be read on our face. If one could ask an intelligence from another world what is the composite expression of the faces of all men, it would without doubt reply, after having seen all men in their joys, in their sorrows, and in their perturbations, "They seem as though thinking of other things." Be great, be wise and eloquent. The soul of the poor man who holds forth his hand at the corner of the bridge will not be jealous, but yours perhaps will envy him his silence. The hero has need of approbation from ordinary men, but the ordinary man does not ask the approbation of heroes, and he pursues his life without uneasiness, as one who has all his treasures in a safe place.

"When Socrates speaks," writes Emerson, "Lysis and Menexenus are afflicted by no shame that they do not speak. They also

48

are good. He likewise defers to them, loves
them whilst he speaks. Because a true and
natural man contains and is the same truth
which an eloquent man articulates, but in
the eloquent man, because he can articulate
it, it seems something the less to reside, and
he turns to these silent, beautiful, with the
more inclination and respect."

Man is eager for explanations. His life
must be shown to him. He rejoices when
he somewhere finds the exact interpretation
of a small gesture which he has been making for some twenty-five years. Here on
earth there is no trivial gesture; there are
in great proportion the attitudes of our
quotidian soul. You will not find in this life
the eternal character of the thought of
Marcus Aurelius. Yet Marcus Aurelius *is*
thought par excellence. Besides, who
among us leads the life of a Marcus
Aurelius? Here, it is the man and nothing

more. He is not arbitrarily exalted; he is merely nearer us than usual. It is John who prunes his tree; it is Peter who builds his house; it is you who speaks to me of the harvest; it is I who give you my hand. But we are so situated that we touch the gods, and we are astonished by what we do. We did not know that all the forces of the soul were present; we did not know that all the laws of the universe were about us, and we turn dumbfounded, like people who have seen a miracle.

Emerson has come to affirm simply this equal and secret grandeur of our life. He has encompassed us with silence and with wonder. He has placed a shaft of light beneath the feet of the workman who leaves the workshop. He has shown us all the powers of heaven and of earth, at the same time intent on sustaining the threshold upon which two neighbours speak of the rain that falls or of the wind that blows.

And above these two passers-by who accost
each other, he has made us see the countenance of God who smiles with the countenance of God. He is nearer than any other
to our common life. He is the most attentive, the most assiduous, the most honest,
the most scrupulous, and probably the most
human of guides. He is the sage of commonplace days, and commonplace days are
in sum the substance of our being. More
than a year passes by without passions,
without virtues, without miracles. Teach
us to respect the little hours of life. If this
morning I have been able to act with the
spirit of Marcus Aurelius, do not over-
emphasise my actions, for I know, even I
myself, that something has happened. But
if I believe I have sacrificed my day to
wretched enterprises, and if you are able
to prove to me that I have lived meanwhile
as profoundly as a hero, and that my soul
has not lost its rights, then you will have

done more than if you had persuaded me
to save my enemy to-day, for you have in-
creased within me the amount, the greatness, and the desire of life; and to-morrow,
in all likelihood, I shall know how to live
with respect.

NOVALIS

I.

"MEN travel by diverse roads; whosoever follows them and compares them will see arise strange figures," writes our author. I have chosen three of these men whose ways lead us upon three different summits. I have seen glimmer on the horizon of Ruysbroeck's works the bluest peaks of the soul, while in Emerson the most humble summits of the human heart round themselves irregularly. Here we find ourselves upon the sharp and often dangerous convolutions of the brain; but there are haunts full of delicious shade between the verdant inequalities of these crests, and the atmosphere there is of an unchangeable crystal.

53

On Emerson and Other Essays

It is splendid to note how many ways of the human soul diverge toward the inaccessible. For an instant, we must follow the steps of the three souls I am about to mention. They went, each in his manner, much further than the sure circles of ordinary consciousness, and each of them met with truths which are not similar and which we nonetheless ought to welcome as prodigal and reclaimed sisters.

A hidden truth is what makes us live. We are its unconscious and silent slaves, and we find ourselves bound so long as it has not appeared. But should one of these extraordinary beings, which are the antennæ of the human soul, many in one, suspect it an instant while groping in the shadows, the humblest amongst us, by an indescribably sudden and inexplicable consequence, feels freed of something. A new truth, higher, purer, and more mysterious, takes the place of that which is discovered and which dis-

54

appears forever, and the soul of all, without anything betraying its presence outwardly, inaugurates a more serene era, and celebrates profound fêtes of the soul, in which we take only a tardy and very remote part. And I believe it is thus that the soul rises, and tends toward a goal of which it alone knows.

All that we can say of it is nothing in itself. Place in one scale of the balance all the words of the wisest men, and in the other the unconscious wisdom of the child yonder who passes, and you will see that what Plato, Marcus Aurelius, Schopenhauer, and Pascal have revealed to us will not outweigh by a line the vast treasures of the unconscious, for the child who is silent is a thousand-fold more wise than Marcus Aurelius who speaks. However, if Marcus Aurelius had not written his twelve books of "Meditations," a part of the unknown treasures our child holds

within him, would not be the same. Perhaps it is not possible to speak clearly of
these things, but those who know how to
question themselves profoundly enough,
and who know how to live—were it only
the fraction of a second and in accordance
with their whole being,—feel that that is.

It is possible that some day we may dis-
cover the reasons why, if Plato, Swedenborg, or Platinus had not existed, the soul
of the peasant, who has never read them
and who has never heard tell of them,
would not be what it infallibly is to-day.
But however that may be, no thought was
ever lost to any soul, and who will tell the
parts of ourselves which live, thanks to the
thoughts which have never been expressed?

Our consciousness has more than one degree, and the wisest take note only of that
part of our consciousness which is almost
unconscious, because it is on the point of becoming divine. To increase this transcen-

56

dental consciousness seems ever to have
been the unknown and supreme desire of
men. It matters little that they are ignorant of it, for they are ignorant of everything; and yet they act in their souls as
wisely as the most wise. It is true that
the majority of men are destined to live only
at the very moment they die. In the mean-
time this consciousness increases only by increasing the inexplicable around us. We
seek to know in order to learn not to know.
We increase only by increasing the mysteries
that weigh us down, and we are slaves
who are only able to keep in them the desire to live on condition of making heavy,
without ever becoming disheartened there-
by, the pitiless weight of their chains. . . .

The history of these wonderful chains
is the unique history of ourselves; for we
are only a mystery, and what we know is
not very interesting. Thus far the history
is not extensive; it is contained in a few

pages, and the best of us, so it is claimed, are afraid to think of it. How few dare advance as far as the limits of human thought; and give us the names of those who remain there a few hours! . . . More than one has promised us the history, and a few others have taken it in hand a moment, but a short while after they lost, step by step, the force that was necessary for them to exist there; they fell back again into their exterior life, into the known fields of human reason, and everything glowed afresh, as formerly, before their eyes.

In truth, that is why it is difficult to question the soul and to recognise the small voice of the child within one, amidst the useless noises around. Yet nevertheless, how little the other efforts of the spirit matter when one thinks of it, and how our ordinary life passes from us! One would say that in the outer world only our fellow-creatures of the empty, distracted, and sterile hours ap-

58

pear.   But here within us is the only fixed
point of our being and the seat itself of life.
We must take refuge there incessantly. We
know all the rest before any one has spoken
to us of it; but here we learn very much
more than can be told; and it is at this moment, when phrases cease and when words
conceal themselves, that our restless eyes
suddenly encounter, through the years and
centuries, another look which lay patiently
in wait for our look on the road to God. ✓
Our eyelids flutter at the same time, the
eyes become moist with a sweet and terrible
dew from the same mystery, and we know
that we are not alone on the endless
road. . . .

But what books speak to us of this place   books
in life?   Metaphysics scarcely touch the
frontiers; and these once passed, in truth
what remains?   A few mystics who seem
mad, because they would probably represent the very nature of man's thought, if

he had the leisure or the force to be a true man. Because we love above all the masters of ordinary reason: Kant, Spinoza, Schopenhauer, and some others,—there is no justification for us to repulse the masters of a different reason—which is an intimate reason as well and which very likely will be our future reason.

In the meanwhile they have told us some indispensable things. Open the most profound of the ordinary moralists or psychologists,—he will speak to you of love, of hatred, of pride, and of the other passions of the heart, and these things please us for an instant, like flowers plucked from their stems. But our real and unalterable life passes a thousand leagues from love and a hundred thousand leagues from pride. We possess a *Self* more profound and more inexhaustible than the *Self* of passions or of pure reason. There is no need to tell us what we experience when our mistress abandons

60

us. She goes away to-day; our eyes weep, but our soul does not weep. Maybe it hears the event and transforms it into light, for all that befalls shines in the soul. Maybe also the soul knows nothing of the event; and if so, what use to speak of it? We must leave such small things to those who do not feel that life is profound.

If I have read La Rochefoucauld or Stendhal this morning, do you believe that I have acquired some thoughts which make me more a man, and that the angels, whom we must approach night and day, will find me more beautiful? Everything that does not go beyond experimental and quotidian wisdom does not belong to us, and is unworthy of our soul. Everything that we are able to learn without anguish lessens us. I will smile regretfully should you succeed in proving to me that I am an egoist even in the sacrifice of my happiness and of my life. But what is egoism compared with so many other all-powerful things I feel living in me with an unspeakable life? It is not upon the threshold of passions that the pure laws of our being are to be found. There comes a moment when the phenomena of habitual consciousness—which could be called passionate consciousness or the consciousness of relations in the first degree,—no longer benefit us, and no longer reach our life. I agree that this consciousness is often interesting in some phase, and that it is essential to know its character. But on the surface it is a plant, whose roots are timid of the great central fire of our being.

I can commit a crime without the least breath disturbing the smallest flame of this fire; and on the other hand a look exchanged, a thought which fails to unfold, a minute which reveals nothing, can stir it in terrible whirlpools to the depths of its retreat, and make it overflow my life. Our soul does not judge as we judge; it is a capricious and hidden thing. It can be touched by a breath, and ignored by a tempest. We must seek for what touches it; the whole matter is there, for it is there that we exist.

Thus, to return to this ordinary consciousness which reigns supreme at so great a distance from our soul, I know more than the one person whom the marvellous picture of Othello's jealousy, for example, no longer astounds. It is determinate in the first circles of man. It remains, provided one takes care to open neither the doors nor the windows; otherwise the image falls into dust in the breath of all the unknown that awaits it outside. We listen to the dialogue between the Moor and Desdemona, as a perfect thing, but it cannot prevent us from thinking of more profound things. Let the warrior from Africa be deceived or not by the noble Venetian, he yet has another life. There must pass in his soul and around his being, at a time coincident with his most miserable suspicions and his most brutal anger, events a thousand times more sublime,—which his cries cannot disturb, —and through the surface emotion of jealousy an unalterable existence is pursued which the genius of man has so far shown only in passing.

Is this the source of the sadness that marks some masterpieces? Poets can write them only on condition of closing their eyes to the terrible horizons, and of imposing silence on the grave and numberless voices of their soul. If they had not done it, they would have lost courage. Nothing is sadder and more elusive than a masterpiece, because nothing reveals better the powerlessness of man to perceive its grandeur and its dignity. And if a voice does not warn us that the most beautiful things are nought beside what we are, nothing will belittle us more.

On Emerson and Other Essays

'The soul," says Emerson [in "The Over-Soul"], "is superior to its knowledge, wiser than any of its works. The great poet makes us feel our wealth, and then we think less of his compositions. His greatest communication to our mind is, to teach us to despise all he has done. Shakespeare carries us to such a lofty strain of intelligent activity, as to suggest a wealth which beggars his own; and we then feel that the splendid works which he has created, and which in other hours we extol as a sort of self-existent poetry, take no stronger hold of real nature than the shadow of a passing traveller on the rock."

The sublime cries of great poems and of great tragedies are nothing more than the mystic cries of anguish which do not belong to the exterior life of these poems or of these tragedies. They resound an instant out from the inner life, and make us hope

On Emerson and Other Essays

I know not what of the unforeseen—and
which we expect, none the less, with so
much impatience! until our passions—too
well-known—cover them once more with
their snow. . . . It is at such moments as
these that humanity is brought for a second
in the presence of itself, as a man is brought
in the presence of an angel. Now, it is important for humanity to place itself as often
as possible in the presence of itself, so as to
know what it is. Should some being of
the other world descend amongst us, and demand of us the supreme flowers of our soul,
and the claims of the earth's greatness,
what would we give him? Some would
bring forward the philosophers without
knowing what they did. I have forgotten
which one has declared that he would offer
Othello, King Lear, and *Hamlet.*

Ah, well, we are not what these are! and
I believe that our soul will die of shame in
the depths of our flesh, because it is well

aware that its visible treasures are not made to be opened to the eyes of strangers, and contains only false precious stones. The most humble amongst us, during the moments of solitude when he knows what is necessary for him to know, feels that he has the right to be represented by something other than a masterpiece. We are in truth invisible beings. We should have nothing to say to the celestial envoy and nothing to show him, and our most beautiful possessions would appear suddenly to us like those poor family relics which seem so precious in the remoteness of their case, but which look so miserable when they are brought forth from their oblivion for a second, in order to show them to some indifferent person.

We are invisible beings who live only within ourselves, and the attentive visitor would go away without ever suspecting what he might have seen, unless in that moment our indulgent soul should intervene. It is so apt to run away from small things, and we have such trouble finding it in life that we fear to call it to our assistance. However, it is ever present, and never deceives itself nor is deceived, once it has been summoned. It would show to the unexpected emissary the clasped hands of man, his eyes so full of nameless dreams, and his lips unable to speak; and perhaps the other, if he be worthy of understanding, would not dare to question. . . .

But if other proofs were necessary to him, the soul would bring him among those whose works almost approach silence. It would open the door of the dwellings where a few loved it for itself, taking account of the small movement of its body. They would both climb to the high solitary plateaus where consciousness rises one degree higher, and where all those who are concerned about themselves prowl attentively around the monstrous circle which binds the apparent world to our superior worlds. The soul would go with him to the limits of mankind; for it is where man seems on the point of finishing that he probably begins; and his essential and indestructible parts find themselves only in the invisible where it is essential for him to keep watch on himself. It is on these heights alone that there are thoughts which the soul can declare, and ideas which resemble the soul and which are as imperious as the soul itself.

It is there that humanity has dwelt an instant, and those peaks, feebly aglow, are probably the only gleams which show the earth in spiritual spaces. Their reflections have truly the colour of our soul. We feel that the passions of the mind and heart resemble, to the eyes of a foreign intelligence, petty village quarrels; but in their works the men of whom I speak have emerged

69

from the smallest village of passions, and
they have said some things that will interest those who are not of this earthly
parish.

Our humanity must not keep up an
agitation exclusively within its innermost
depths, like a horde of moles. Let it
live as though some day it should render account of its life to its elder brothers. The
mind alone contemplates itself, like a local
celebrity which makes the traveller smile.
There are other things than the mind, and
it is not the mind alone which allies us to
the universe. It is time to confound it no
longer with the soul. What is essential for
us to consider is not what takes place as
between men, but what has place within us
above the passions of reason. If I offer to
a foreign intelligence only La Rochefoucauld, Lichtenberg, Meredith, or Stendhal,
it would regard me as I regard, in the
depths of a dead town, the hopeless bour-

geois who speaks to me of his street, of his marriage, and of his business.

What angel will demand of Titus why he has not married Berenice and why Andromaque is promised to Pyrrus? What will Berenice amount to, if I compare her to what is invisible in the beggar-woman who stops me or in the prostitute who beckons me? A mystic word only can now and then represent a human being; but our soul does not exist in these other regions without shadows and without abysses. And do you yourselves stop there in the grave hours when life is heavy on your shoulder? Man is not in these things, and yet these things are perfect. But one must speak of them only to one's self, and it is right to remain silent concerning them if some visitor knocks one evening at the door. Yet if this same visitor should surprise me at the moment when my soul is looking for the key to her nearest treasures in Pascal, Emerson,

or Hello, or, on the other hand, in some
one of those who were concerned about
pure beauty, I will not close the book in
embarrassment; and perhaps he himself
will take therefrom some idea of an intimate being condemned to silence, or will
know at least that we were not all contented inhabitants of the earth.

II

Among these envoys of the human soul,
Novalis probably represents one of the
most imponderable, one of the most subtle,
and one of the most transparent aspects of
the superior being silent within the depths
of us. He is the strolling soul, the crystalline bee of this almost immovable group.
He is likewise a mystic as the others, but his
mysticism is of a special kind. "What is
mysticism?" he asks himself in one of his
fragments, "And what should be treated

72

mystically? Religion, love, politics. All lofty things have some connection with mysticism. If all men were only a couple of lovers, the difference between mysticism and non-mysticism would be at an end."

Between a mystic thought and an ordinary thought, however exalted it may be, there is the same difference as between the dead eyes of the blind and those of the child who beholds the mountain and the sea. The soul of man never errs here. The question is not alone of mysticism, theological or ecstatic. All who perceive things beyond the customary phenomena of passion or reason are themselves mystics also. Had Pascal aided Racine while he wrote "Berenice," the lovers of Berenice would have been mystic—that is to say more human—and Pascal would have put there an indescribable something which would have recalled the look of the loved one at the moment when her eyes encountered those of

73

her lover. And the poem would have been inexhaustible. Instead of which Berenice now lives a dry and detached life which will never be renewed. Berenice is undying, but she does not, like Hamlet and Cordelia, commune with God.

There are a thousand diverse mysticisms. "Mysticism," says Matter, the biographer of Claude de Saint-Martin, "has gone further than positive science and rational speculation, and has as many diverse forms as there are eminent mystics. But beneath all its forms it has two ambitions which are the same: to arrive in metaphysical studies as far as intuition, and in moral practice as far as perfection. The highest science and the highest morality:—this in two words is what it looks for, what it has the determined will to conquer, and the pretension if not to teach—for its conquests teach little—at least to let see imperfectly."

Novalis does not concern himself expressly with theosophy, with magic, with transcendental pneumatology, with metaphysical cosmology, or with all we find in the spacious circles of the mystic, properly speaking. He is an almost unconscious mystic who has no aim. He thinks mystically, since a thought which communicates in a certain fashion with the infinite is a mystic thought. We must everywhere seek for thoughts of this kind, for they are the only ones in which our soul truly lives. And as these thoughts are very rare, we must be contented with the slightest efforts and attempts. I do not mean to say that Novalis is a supremely admirable being. His teaching is very vague, and he does not advance any new solution to the great questions of being. But some of his thoughts are undoubtedly impregnated with the special odour of our soul, and you recognise without trouble this odour that no language can ever define. He has found a way to clothe a

75

certain number of earthly things in mystic
vestments; and these are the calmest, the
most spontaneous, and the most virginal
vestments one can encounter. His mysticism
is even so natural and so essential that we
do not see it at the outset.

In him, infinite communications are
formed before you realise it, and extend
over all with grace. He does not torture
himself; he does not search in shadows or
in tears, but he smiles at things with a
gentle indifference, and regards the world
with the inattentive curiosity of an angel,
unoccupied and distraught by long memories. He plays simply in the gardens of
the soul, without suspecting that he has
reached the extreme end of life, and that he
often passes his hands between the branches
to pluck the flowers from the other side of
the burning hedge.

He is also very far from the exuberant
and obscure joy of the ascetic mystic. He

On Emerson and Other Essays

does not feel the intolerable flames that
melt souls at the opposite poles of divine
love. He is rather an astonished and sweet-
voiced child who possesses the sense of
unity. He is not sad and he is not restless.
"There is not, properly speaking, any unhappiness in this world," he tells us; and
yet he was as unhappy as any other man.
But unhappiness could not sink into his
soul, nor did it succeed in troubling his
thoughts.

"Sorrow is a divine vocation," he says
again; but one feels that he has not known
sorrow, and that he speaks of it as a traveller who has not fathomed the language of
a country through which he passes. Do
what it may, the soul is the sister of sorrow
or of joy, and events are not able to work
any change in it. When his little sweetheart died—the only woman he truly loved
—his life seemed broken. He did no more
than weep dreamily upon her grave. At

77

what point in his work did she die? That is
very difficult to say; and, in spite of all his
tears, the angelic optimism of his life could
not become darkened;—so true is it that
we know but a few things concerning the
laws of the soul, and that our life has no
action on it.

Besides, he does not concern himself with
anything that is certain. He lives in the
domain of erratic intuitions, and nothing is
more elusive than his philosophy. His
mysticism, to use one of his expressions
which he loves and which he often employs
when he speaks of his science, is rather "a
magic idealism." It seems to him that nothing is more within reach of the spirit than
the infinite, and that is why he scarcely ever
enters the ordinary field of human thoughts.
He only wanders over the frontiers of this
thought, but he goes over nearly all of
them.

With the greater number of mystics

known to us, mysticism is psychological;
that is to say, it attaches itself to a species
of transcendental psychology where the
soul itself endeavours to study its own
habits and passions, as our mind, in ordinary psychology, endeavours to study the
passions and habits of our being, apart from
mystery. The immovable soul falls back
upon itself and concerns itself less with the
unknown which lies about it than with the
unknown which lies within; or rather, it perceives accidentally the exterior mystery only
through and in relation to the inner mystery. In general, it is mystic only in respect to itself, whereas, in Novalis, the soul
may be mystic in its relation to a chemical
phenomena, a pathological law, or an arith-
metical problem.

The soul shifts position every moment,
and finds itself again everywhere outside of
itself. Instead of drawing within it the
externals and appearances, the soul mixes

itself with them and so saturates them with its essence that it changes their substance. It transcendentalises less its own *Self* than the universe. It enters art, science, and morals; and this art, science, and morals are no longer what they were and no longer directly belong to present life.

Moreover, we do not know how to define better than Novalis has done, illusive nature and the particular origin of his spiritual emotions. "There are in all of us," he writes, "certain thoughts which seem to have a character entirely different from others, for they are accompanied by a sensation of fatality; yet nevertheless, there is no outward reason for them to be born. It seems that we take part in a dialogue, and that some unknown and spiritual being gives us in a strange manner the opportunity of developing the most obvious thoughts. This being must be superior since it enters *en rapport* with us in a way impossible to those beings bound to phenomena. This being must be homogeneous with us, since it treats us as spiritual beings, and only very rarely calls us to personal activity. This superior *Self* is to man what man is to nature, or what the sage is to the child. Man endeavours to become like unto it, as he endeavours to become similar to the *not-Self*. It is impossible to establish this fact; each of us must experience it for himself. This is a fact of superior order that superior man alone can grasp, but the others endeavour to bring it out in themselves. Philosophy is an auto-logician of superior essence, an auto-manifestation: the excitation of the real *Self* by the ideal *Self*. Philosophy is the foundation of all the other manifestations, and the determination to philosophise is the invitation made by the real *Self* to take consciousness, to awaken itself, and to become spirit."

It would be difficult, concerning the

thought with which we are here occupied, and which goes beyond the first circles of the soul, to find a notion more acceptable than that which in passing we here en- counter: "Philosophy,"—and Novalis means to speak only of transcendental philosophy,—"is an excitation of the real *Self* by the ideal *Self.*" As for the nature of his thoughts, he determines this better than the most skilful commentator would, when he says: "that they [the thoughts] are accompanied by a sensation of fatality, and that an unknown being gives him in a strange fashion the opportunity to develop the most obvious among them."

The evidence of which he speaks is more- over this fugitive evidence which we per- ceive only at the most lucid hours of life. But what we see only at long intervals, ob- scurely and without our realising, without any other thing revealing it to us to save an unknown satisfaction and an indefinable increase of a general force, he perceives every day, and succeeds in holding fast to a part of what he perceives.

If we must characterise Novalis by a word, we might say that he was a scientific mystic, though he only concerned himself with science at moments, and at places where it was on the point of being confounded with poetry. "There is a divining atmosphere," he says somewhere; and he is the one of those who come forth the most rarely out of this precious atmosphere. He catches a glimpse continually, on the extreme limits of the plausible, of many things of which there is no proof, but which we ourselves are nevertheless unable to refrain from recognising and admiring. He touches upon them only in passing; and before you have had time to recover from your astonishment, he awaits you, all smiles, on the most solitary cape of the other hemisphere.

Novalis has those eyes which for an instant bind all worlds together. Perhaps he is the one who has most profoundly penetrated intimate and mystic nature and the secret unity of the universe. He has the sense and the very sweet torment [meaning that he chafes under the thought] of unity. "He sees nothing isolated," and above all things he is the doctor who looks in amazement at the mysterious relations existing between all things. He gropes without cessation at the extremes of this world, where the sun only rarely shines, and on every side he suspects and touches lightly upon strange coincidences and astounding analogies, obscure, trembling, fugitive, and timid, which vanish before one has understood.

But he has caught a glimpse of a certain number of things one would never have suspicioned, had he not gone so far. He is the clock that has marked some of the most subtle hours of the human soul. It is evident that he has more than once been mistaken; but despite the winds of folly and of error whirling around him, he has been able to maintain himself a longer time than any other on the dangerous peaks where all is at the point of being lost. He seems to be the hesitant consciousness of unity, but the most vaguely complete that we have had thus far. And there are few human beings in whom our universe was more spiritualised and more divinely human. He is like the serene master of Saïs: "He hears, sees, touches, and thinks at the same time. Often, the stars seem to him like men; then again men seem to him like the stars, stones like animals, clouds like plants. He plays with forces and phenomena."

III

Friedrich von Hardenberg, who in literature took the name of "Novalis," was born, May 2, 1772, in the old family residence of

Weidestedt, in the ancient county of Mans-
field, Saxony. His father, who had been a
soldier in youth, and who was an honest and
solid German,—who, moreover, never understood anything of the genius of his son,
was director of the Saxony salt-works—an
important employment at that time,—
which assured a very large independence to
his household.

His mother, of whom little is said, according to custom, though mothers create
the soul of beings, was in all likelihood one
of those sweet and pious women who, passing through life without explaining to herself the attitude of man, contents herself by
remaining silent and by hiding what she
knows and divines, beneath a poor, humble
smile. It is possible that Novalis had
memories of her in describing the simple
and tender woman who accompanied his
hero, Henry of Ofterdingen, in his ideal
voyage.

86

On Emerson and Other Essays

It was with her and with his three sisters that Novalis passed, in this small, lonely chateau, the whole of his delicate childhood. He lived there, within the rooms of the old German dwelling—rooms slightly sombre and crowded—that discreet and silent life which allows the inner being time to find itself and to question itself from the first hours. Then he studied at the universities of Jena, Leipzig, and Wittenberg, and now we have come to the time when, having passed those obscure years through which the soul unconsciously makes ready, —and when it is about to enter those paths of light traced by his work upon his life,— he does the small things of which lives are made.

The year is 1794. Thirteen years have passed since Kant published his "Critique of Pure Reason"; but not more than four or five years have elapsed since this book spread in Germany and began, with enthusiasm and anger, the despotic reign of the philosopher of Koenigsberg. While Kant analyses, Fichte at the same time reconstructs the world in his "Doctrine of Sciences," while Schelling, in his small room at Leipzig, already teaches to those disciples among whom was Novalis, the absolute identity of the objective and of the subjective.

It is not the place here to recall, *apropos* of a rather literary philosophy, the great quarrels of the golden age in German metaphysics. It suffices that we know the youth of Novalis was passed, even in the very centre of this vast conflagration of human thought. But never did he enter into the narrow prisons of systematic philosophy. He loved better to imagine the world according to the free transports of his soul than to limit it to the exigencies of a first idea, irrevocable and arbitrary. He had genius, and Kane has

88

declared that genius has no place in science.

Of the three great philosophers who then governed human thought, it is certain that Fichte, the passionate thinker, left the most profound impressions on his mind; and he often recalls him in his writings. It is, nevertheless, impossible to know exactly the influence they had upon the soul of Novalis, for the true inner life depends on those small circumstances which can never be known. Goethe, in his spiritual autobiography, speaks of none of the large events of his life, but devotes many long pages to the humble games of his childhood. The soul never listens, but it sometimes hears, and should we go to the sources of our new and definitive existence, we would often find there the word of a drunkard, of a maid, or of a prostitute, even where the wisest among our masters have spoken in vain.

Besides, the philosopher never remains

long among his brothers. "Philosophy," Novalis writes somewhere, "rests at this moment in my library. I am happy in having traversed this labyrinth of pure reason, and in having dwelt anew, body and soul, within the refreshing countries of the senses. . . . One can place philosophy very high without making it the director of his house, and without resigning one's self to live solely for it. Mathematics alone do not make the soldier and mechanic; so, philosophy alone will not make a man."

At the same time we find ourselves within the great literary century of Germany. Goethe, who is so difficult to define, the man with a thousand aptitudes, the Argus who smiles gravely upon all inner truth, is about to give "Faust" to the world, and is on the eve of publishing "Wilhelm Meister." And "Wilhelm Meister," that illusive and inexhaustible book of all books, influences Novalis till his death. He did not like it, yet he returned to it incessantly. He was obsessed by it, and could no longer forsake it. In the diary for the last years of his life, the most important event of the morning or of the evening was daily the impatient and discontented adoration of the "Meister." He loved it and detested it at the same time, as one loves and detests a mistress to whom a mysterious and wretched law attaches you. This was the book of his life, and one could say of it that it weighed heavily upon his entire existence. He wrestled vainly against "the angel of romantic irony"; he contradicted it and repulsed it; and the instant after, he fell again into its arms, his eyes closed in admiration. He knew, nevertheless, the faults of this breviary of daily life. "It is entirely modern and prosaic," he tells us. The romantic perishes here just as the poesy of nature and the marvellous. It speaks only of ordinary things. Artistic atheism—that is the spirit of the book." But "the ardent and sainted Novalis," as Emerson calls him, was not able, amidst the greatest sorrows of his life, to forget for an instant this *Candide* directed against poetry, which till his last days possessed his soul with the memory of his dead sweetheart.

Around Goethe all Germany flourished. We know the history of the Romantic School. So as to picture the *milieu* in which his life flowed, it suffices only to know that, still very young,—almost a child —Novalis turned quite often to the great and tender Schiller, and never forgot the ecstasy in which those delicious hours steeped him. He was an intimate friend of the two Schlegels, whose beautiful translations introduced Shakespeare to Germany. He was also the friend of the enormous Jean-Paul, so little known in France—Jean-Paul, the romantic and mystic Rabelais of the Germans, the

most powerful, the most slovenly, the most
inexhaustible, the most chaotic and the
most gentle of literary monsters. Then,
toward his final days, it was Ludwig Tieck,
the good and faithful Tieck of artless and
limpid legends, who set about earnestly at-
tempting, with Schlegel, to collect the works
of this child whom death had impatiently
seized.

But, as yet, death was at the turn of the
road. Novalis had finished his law studies.
He likewise applied himself to chemistry
and to mathematics. He left Wittenberg
and installed himself at Tennstedt. Henceforward, the several years set aside for the
accomplishment of his work were passed
between Tennstedt, Weissenfels, and Grüningen in Thuringia. Destiny, who knows
what must be done, and who draws from
some men of interest to her all that can be
drawn, places him in the small, drowsy,
familiar and patriarchal town of central

Germany. It is easy to picture the sur-
roundings. There are great trees; generally
pines all about, and mountains, the metal-
bearing Erzgebirge. The Harz and the
great Thuringia forest are near. The vine
thrives on the banks of the Saale. The inhabitants work in the salt-mines and in the
copper-mines. There are some old, squat
inns, under linden trees, by the wayside;
some towers in ruins upon the cliffs; and
all the dark and green confused, yet nonetheless familiar; leaning houses, moss-
grown stubble and slightly blackened chateaux of legendary Germany. The people
gather the harvest, singing the while about
the sheaves. They pass the small bridge
over the streamlet in the forest; they return
to the village at mid-day and in the evening: and life, as everywhere under the sun
or stars, flows in expectancy.

In 1776, just at the very moment his
days were ironically numbered, the poet,

94

equipped in so many things, prepared to live in the full exercise of his powers. He entered into the administration of the Saxony salt-mines. But some months previously, the greatest event of his pure and simple life took place by chance, without noise and without attracting attention, like all events which penetrate the soul.

It was during a visit to Thuringia, in which his good friend Just accompanied him—Just who later became his astonished and vague biographer. I leave the word to Ludwig Tieck, whose narrative still trembles beneath the fresh-coloured hue of this first love:

"He arrived at Cronstadt not long ago, when in a neighbouring country-house he became acquainted with Sophie von Kühn. The first glance he threw upon the beautiful and marvellous apparition decided his life. We can even say that the sentiment which now penetrated him and inspired him was the substance and the essence of his entire life. Often in the look and features of a child, there is an expression which we are compelled to call superhuman or celestial, since it is of a very angelic and ethereal beauty. And usually when we see countenances thus purified and made almost transparent, the fear comes to us that they are too fragile, too delicately fashioned for this life; that death or immortality looks upon us very profoundly in those sparkling eyes. And often a rapid decay transforms our sad presentiment to certitude. These countenances are indeed more impressive still when their first period is happily over, and when they offer themselves to us on the flowering threshold of their adolescence. Every one who had known this marvellous betrothed of our friend agrees that no description is able to convey an idea of the grace and celestial harmony in which this beautiful being moved, of the beauty which shone in her, of the sweetness and the majesty which surrounded her. Novalis became the poet each time he spoke of her. She had just ended her thirteenth year when he saw her for the first time. The spring and summer of the year 1795 were the flower of his life. Every hour he was able to steal away from his duties, he passed at Grüningen; and at the close of this same year, he obtained from Sophie's parents the desired consent."

It is probable that the old poet had seen the small sweetheart only through the ecstasy of his friend. However, it matters very little into what vase man pours the illusions of love, and I believe that Tieck exaggerates the influence this encounter had on the life and thought of Novalis. In such men thought is a sumptuous and central plant which protected, rises above all

circumstances. And then, generally, the soul
follows its way as a blind man who does not
allow himself to be distracted by the flowers
of the road. If, in passing, the soul sees
another soul, it is because this other soul already travels the same paths. And our
inner being is almost unshakable. Every
work by Novalis, written before and after
the loss of Sophie von Kühn, has the happy
elasticity of days of pure delirium, of sweet
and infinite love. It was in him that love
itself dwelt, and the object of his affection
was only an occasion. But really at heart
one does not know. Many very vital events
often emanate from the woman, and she
frequently changes the direction of a life.
But is it, indeed, the woman—because she is
the woman, who had the influence, and is it
not rather a soul that has intervened? It
happens, moreover, that a life is changed
without the soul having moved. Yet it is
possible that the woman's soul had an action

more prompt than that of the man, or it is possible that we remark it more. However that may be, this extraordinary maid of thirteen years was, as you will see, similar to all maidens of her age. She spoke, she laughed, she smoothed her hair, she ate green fruit, and she still played with what remained of her dolls. We find in Novalis's last note-books a page of ingenious memoranda, wherein he admires her small gestures and her little school-girl thoughts, without suspecting that everyone has made those gestures and has had those thoughts since the beginning of the world. He notes reverently that she "likes vegetable soup, beef and French beans, just as she likes beer and wine. She is afraid of a mouse and of a spider. She is afraid of ghosts. She fears marriage. She loves passionately all that is proper for her to love. They sometimes beat her. She is irritable and tenderhearted. Novalis's love often tires her. She

note

is cold. She is an excellent housekeeper.
All alone she tried one day to stop a thief.
She loves to listen to stories. She is extraordinarily insincere." "Women are more
complete than we," he adds, "more proud
than we. They are more intuitive than we.
Their nature seems to be our art, and our
nature their art. They individualise; we
universalise. . . ."

Here then she is—such as he loved; and
we see her a second with his eyes,—a
maiden similar to those you find in all well-
to-do houses and in the parlours of all board-
ing-schools. It was she whom he loved and
admired, and it was because of her that he
died. He was perhaps right, and that is not
astonishing. Undoubtedly he knew, without being able to confess it to himself, what
there was in her. And if he adored her
little insignificant gestures, it was because
he was not ignorant of the fact that a more

profound being surely lay awake in the
depths of her commonplace smiling eyes.
One never knows what these lover's en-
counters hold. Besides, we can never judge
of a woman by what is left of her acts, of
her thoughts, or by what is said of her. It
is necessary to have seen her, and to have
approached her, so as to know what she is
and what the unknown being is worth
which lives within her. For woman, more
than man, is a question of soul.

He was happy during all one spring, during all one summer. But misfortune awaited
him, all smiles, on the threshold of the
dying year. The little Sophie fell suddenly and seriously ill. An abscess formed
in the liver, and her poor virgin flesh was
handed over to the scalpel of the doctors.
The year following, Novalis passed by
wandering from the paternal house, where
one of his brothers lay dying, to the cot-
tage at Grüningen, where his young be-

trothed was at the point of death. Finally,
on March 19, 1797, Sophie von Kühn
gave up the dream or life. She was fifteen.
Three weeks after, Novalis's brother in his
turn expired.

It is not necessary to speak at length of
sorrow. All that there is of an exterior
sorrow varies according to the days in
which we live, and what it possesses of an
inner quality can neither be weighed nor
spoken of. What was at first violent in
Novalis was transformed later into a
strange peace, saddened and profound, and
the grave and penetrating cold of true life
rose out of the depths of his misfortune.
He was as a drunken man who one evening in winter awakens under the stars at
the summit of a tower. From that day forth
he smiled profoundly and his dead sweetheart began in him a pure and solemn life.
Nothing is more nobly sad than this transformation of sorrow at the depths of a soul,

though nothing perhaps could be less rare. But the majority of souls are silently submissive, and we are surrounded by a crowd of mute and solitary beauties.

He lived thus with this invisible loved one. I will quote here a page from his intimate diary—a page which I have taken at random—for they all resemble each other, and, as one remarks frequently at the approach of death, his life became serene and monotonous.

"May 5.—Forty-eight days after the death of Sophie. Early, as of habit, thought of her. Afterwards, reflections upon criticism. Then 'Meister.' After the meal, lively political discussions. Walk. On the way, happy and profound meditations, notably on this remark of Goethe's: that rarely do we know and choose the proper means towards the end; that very rarely do we take the right way. It seems

that I am becoming better and more profound. Of late, I have had a most vivid
image of her before me: in profile, at my
side on the sofa; with a green kerchief. It
is in such situations and characteristic vestments that I like to remember her most frequently. All the evening, thought of her
very intimately. God, so far, has guided
me charitably. He will continue to do so."

And the diary runs thus during three
months, detailing with regularity the same
recollections and the same small deeds:
walks, work, meals, small fêtes, visits to the
tomb of Sophie, music under the linden-
trees, and evenings under the lamp. "So-
cial life becomes more and more foreign to
me, and things more and more indifferent,"
he remarks; and the next day he rejoices as
a child in a beautiful, sunny day, for life in
spite of all is more powerful than memory.
Among the insignificant facts, he examines

himself and deliberates: "I have remarked that it is my destiny in this world never to attain anything. It is necessary that I separate myself from everything in its prime, and only at the end shall I learn the best in what I know well. Even myself. . . . It is only now that I have learned to know myself and to find pleasure in myself. And that is why I must go from the world."

He often speaks of a fixed resolution. He questions what emptiness his death would make in his family, and realises that no being is indispensable. When he is with his friends he speaks more than once of suicide. The idea of putting an end to his days—was it floating in his mind? He does not say so. The notes continue almost daily, until the one hundred and second day after Sophie's death. Then suddenly, on turning one of the pages, there shines forth the name of another woman.

Novalis, in 1798, had gone to Freyberg, in order to study mineralogy under the illustrious Werner. There he met a young girl, Julie von Charpentier, and the new betrothments were celebrated a short while after.

Here, all biographers are frightened away. The good Tieck stammers with excuses, and the old Just passes rapidly by without daring to look. Carlyle himself, even though accustomed to the unlooked-for movements of true heroes, is embarrassed a moment, and separates active constancy from passive constancy, which is, he says, a very inferior virtue, an accident rather than a virtue, and in every particular very rare in this world. "His Sophie," he adds, "might still be a saintly presence, mournful and unspeakably mild, to be worshipped in the inmost shrine of his memory; but worship of this sort is not man's sole business; neither should we censure Novalis that he dries his tears, and once more looks abroad with hope on the earth, which is still as it was before, the strangest complex of mystery and light, of joy as well as sorrow. 'Life belongs to the living; and he that lives must be prepared for vicissitudes.' " I do not believe that we should offer many explanations, and I should love Novalis less had he not loved twice. It is necessary to live naïvely, and *ok* the dead have other rights over us.

Now, the happy days returned, sunnier and more beautiful than formerly. He had obtained important employment in Thuringia, his life enlarged itself, and his second fiancée awaited him, smiling in the sweet impatience of betrothal. Never had he felt nearer to him the warm and powerful presence of good fortune. We must not take too seriously this sensation of plenitude, of strength, of hope and of joy, even as we do not trust death. It is the instructive and supreme reaction of life which knows all, against misfortune which draws near and will land to-morrow. If we feel our good fortune most vividly, it is because sorrow in passing touches us on the shoulder in order to bid us farewell. Suddenly, during the summer of 1800, just at the moment when all his joys were about to be realised, the unexpected death of one of his brothers troubled him so profoundly that a blood-vessel broke in his chest; he bled profusely. He was carried to Dresden, then to Weissenfels, where he dragged on for some time amidst great hope and brilliant projects, in the manner of consumptives, and died on March 25, 1801. He had not completed his twenty-ninth year.

IV

I shall pass rapidly in review, so as to end this study, the works of Novalis, which, in the original edition, accompany the fragments here translated: "Henry of Ofterdingen," which is at the beginning of the collection by Tieck and Schlegel, was written in Thuringia, in the solitudes of the "golden meadow," at the foot of the Kyffhaüserbergs. It was in 1800, and Novalis, on the verge of death, and engaged a second time, full of hope, of projects, and of ardour, smiled at existence with a joy and a confidence which till then he had never experienced. "Henry of Ofterdingen" was intended by him to be the positive of which "Wilhelm Meister" was the negative that had weighed upon all his youth. He desired a kind "of apotheosis of poetry." As a complete translation of this novel must appear before long, I will dispense with an analysis here.

This work, which he had not the time to finish, is the most continuous and the most considerable effort of our author. But one will not find here the astonishing and happy audacity of the "Fragments." The artist in "Ofterdingen" wrestles with the thinker, and their powers are weakened at moments in the struggle. This is a monochrome work, clear, cold, beautiful and noble. But the pure essence of the genius of Novalis appears to a less degree here than elsewhere. From the beginning to the end, there is to be found, nevertheless, that marvellous crystalline clarity which is his very own, and which manifests itself especially in this book—a book which some one has said was written by an angel descended from some paradise of snow and ice.

Following this, we have the "Hymns to Night." It is a brief series of poems in prose and in verse, written shortly after the death of his fiancée. Novalis regarded these poems as the most perfect part of his work. "They are," writes Carlyle, "of a strange, veiled, almost enigmatical character; nevertheless, more deeply examined, they appear nowise without true poetic worth; there is a vastness, an immensity of idea; a still solemnity reigns in them, a solitude almost as of extinct worlds. Here and there, too, some light-beam visits us in the void deep; and we cast a glance, clear and wondrous, into the secrets of that mysterious soul."

. . . Here is one of these poems:

"The morning—will it ever return? and the effort of the earth—will it never end? Evil activity consumes the celestial breath of the night. The secret oblation of love —will it never burn eternally? Time is measured by light, but the reign of night knows neither time nor space. Eternal is

the duration of sleep. Sacred sleep! do not
make too rarely happy those who are dedi-
cated to the night in their earthly works!
The madman alone disowns you, and
knows no other sleep than the shadow you
spread so mercifully upon us in this twi-
light of the true night. They do not feel
you in the golden flood of grapes, in the
marvellous oil of the almond, and in the
tawny vigor of the poppy. They do not
know that it is you who envelops the
bosom of the virgin, and makes a paradise
of her knees. They do not suspect that
from the depths of legends you advance in
half-opening the sky, and that you carry the
key of the dwelling of happiness; silent
messenger of infinite secrets."

Novalis is also the author of a series of
"Spiritual Hymns," destined to be sung in
the churches; and of some other poems
which I shall only mention here so as to be
complete. These "Spiritual Hymns" have

the clear and sweet harmony, the purity and
the strange transparency which characterise
the genius of the poet, but there is no need
to look here for what he himself calls "the
core of his soul."

We next find, in the Tieck collection,
"The Disciples at Saïs," the admirable
physical, or rather metaphysical, novel, of
which a complete translation has been
made. There are few works more myste- *Saïs*
rious, more serene, and more beautiful. It
has been said that he climbed I know not
what interior mountain known only to himself; and that from the height of this silent
summit he saw at his feet, nature, systems,
hypotheses, and the thoughts of men. He
does not summarise, he purifies; he does
not judge, he dominates without saying
anything. In those very profound and
solemn dialogues, intermingled with sym- *note*
bolical allusions, which stretch occasionally
much beyond possible thought, he has fixed

113

the remembrance of one of the soul's most lucid instants. It suffices that the reader be cautioned that he is here concerned with one of those rare books, where each, in accordance with his merits, finds his reward. Unfortunately the work is incomplete. From the beginning, the author has overlept the narrow confines of ordinary forces, and he has been able, for a longer time than any other, to deviate from it. But one evening, it became quite necessary for him to halt in his journey before he could describe what he had already seen; for there is an abyss between what one is able to say and what one discovers. Later on, in his numberless papers, there were found the notes which are here reproduced and which seem to refer to some project interrupted either by awe or death. What there is of it, I here transcribe:

"Transformation of the Temple of

Saïs. Apparition of Isis. Death of the
Master. Dream in the Temple. Studio of
Archæus. Advent of the Greek gods. *note*
Initiation into the mysteries. Statue of
Memnon. Journey to the pyramids. The
Child and his forerunner. The Messiah of
nature. The New Testament and the new
nature. The New Jerusalem. Cosmogony
of the ancients. Hindu divinities."

Let us now leave the fragments of this
mysterious work which oblivion seems to
fret on every side, so as to reach some other
fragments, even more mutilated still,—for
the whole work of this unfortunate poet is
an ideal monument which fatality made
into marvellous ruins before it was built. It ✓ good
has been said of Novalis, *apropos* of these
"Fragments," that he was a German Pascal, and the phrase, in some respects, may
be regarded as quite just. Certainly he
has not the clear and profound power, the

ponderous force, and the prodigious elasticity of the great wild beast in "Thoughts;" he is a Pascal, slightly somnambulistic, who only very rarely enters the realm of certitudes, where he takes delight in his brother.

But there are some things as beautiful as certitudes. Pascal had not known Boehme, Lavater, Eckartshausen, Zinzendorf, Yung, Stilling; and the great Boehme notably never relinquished the splendid booty that he seized. Novalis dwells in the realm of hypotheses and of uncertainty; and the power of man becomes hesitant in those regions. He does not possess the purpose of Pascal; he goes in a circle, his eyes bandaged in the desert; but it is necessary to recognise that his range is immense. He wished to accomplish a kind of encyclopedic work, wherein the experiences and the ideas born of the most diverse sciences would be mutually cleared, sustained, and verified, he tells us. He probably would never have been able to achieve this work, but the scattered remains of it are beautiful and strange.

A large proportion of these "Fragments" has been collected by Schlegel and Tieck in the volume which contains the other works of the poet. In 1846, Ludwig Tieck, aided by Edouard von Bülow, published a new series of "Fragments" which did not even then exhaust the enormous mass of notes left by the author of "The Disciples at Saïs." In my turn, I have made a choice from these selections. Novalis, in his work, touches upon most of the human sciences. I have set aside a certain number of political considerations which now no longer offer any interest. I have also discarded everything that the advance in physics and chemistry has made out of date or erroneous. I have done the same in regard to certain historical questions which bore almost exclusively on the situation in Germany at the time the author wrote.

As for the rest, the choice was more difficult and arbitrary; for it was necessary to limit myself at present. Besides, it is possible that a second volume may complete this work. I am able to assert, however, that among these Thoughts, I have gathered those which are impregnated with the true and pure essence of Novalis's genius, whatever the repugnance they have to tell their secret. I close by hoping that the reader will pardon inevitable errors. It is not easy to translate into French an obscure author who occasionally seems to speak in a low tone. Our language is a minute and severe interpreter, which, before agreeing to interpret anything, requires construing, which it is often very dangerous to give it.

RUYSBROECK

I

A great number of books are more regularly beautiful than this by Ruysbroeck the Admirable. A great number of mystics are more effective and more timely: Swedenborg and Novalis, among many. It is most likely that his writings only rarely meet the needs of the present. On the other hand, I know of few authors more clumsy; at times he loses himself in strange possibilities; and the first twenty chapters of the "Ornament of Spiritual Marriages," although probably a necessary preparation, contain only a few indifferent and pious, commonplace premises. Externally he has no order, no scholastic logic. He often repeats himself, and seems at times to con-

tradict himself. He joins the ignorance of
a child to the science of some one who might
have just returned from the dead. He has
a rabid syntax, which has troubled me more
than once. He introduces an image and
forgets it. He even employs a certain number of unrealisable images; and this phenomenon, abnormal in a sincere work, can
be explained only by his awkwardness and
by his extraordinary haste. He is ignorant
of most of the artifices of speech, and can
only discuss the inexpressible. He is ignorant of nearly every practice, every qualifi-
cation, every resource of philosophic
thought; and he is compelled to think only
of the inconceivable.

When he speaks to us of his small mo-
nastic garden, he can hardly and sufficiently
tell us what is happening there. Then he
writes as a child would write. He under-
takes to inform us of what takes place in
God, and he writes many pages that Plato

could not have written. In every part there is an absurd disproportion between science and ignorance, between force and desire. We must not expect a literary work; you will perceive nothing more than the convulsive flight of a tipsy eagle, blind and blood-stained above snowy summits.

I will add a final word in the manner of a fraternal warning. I have had occasion to read some books which are considered very abstruse: the "Disciples of Saïs" and the "Fragments" of Novalis, for instance; the "Biographia Literaria" and the "Friend" by Samuel Taylor Coleridge; the "Timæus" of Plato; the "Enneads" by Plotinus; Saint-Denys the Areopagite's "Divine Names"; and the "Aurora" by the great German mystic, Jacob Boehme, with whom our author has a closer analogy.

I would not venture to say that the works of Ruysbroeck are more abstruse than these books, but we are less prone to pardon his

abstruseness, since here we are concerned
with an unknown in which from the beginning we have no confidence. It seems to
me essential that we frankly anticipate the
casual reader on the threshold of this
shapeless temple: for the present translation has only been undertaken for the satisfaction of a few Platonists. I believe
that those who have not dwelt in the inti-
macy of Plato and of the neo-Platonists of
Alexandria will not proceed very far in the
perusal of this. They will imagine themselves in a desert; they will have the sensation of a uniform fall into a fathomless
abyss, between black, smooth walls.

In this book there is neither ordinary
light nor air; and it is a spiritual abode in-
supportable to those not prepared for it.
We must not regard it out of literary
curiosity; there are few bric-à-bracs in it.
The spiritual botanists will not find here any
more flowers than they would find on ice-

bergs at the pole. I tell them that this is a limitless desert, where ordinary readers will die of thirst. They will find here few phrases which we, in the manner of literary lovers, might examine and admire; they are either jets of flame or blocks of ice. Do not look for roses upon this Iceland. Maybe some solitary corollo awaits between two icebergs; there are, in fact, some strange explosions, some unknown expressions, some unheard-of resemblances, but none of them pays for the time consumed in coming from so far to cull them. We must, before entering here, be in a philosophic state as different from the ordinary state as wakefulness differs from sleep.

Porphyry, in his "Principles of the Theory of Comprehensibles," seems to have written the most appropriate warning to place at the head of this book: "Through intelligence one says many things of the source [moral law] which is superior to intelligence. But one is possessed with an intuitive knowledge of it much better by an absence of thought than by thought itself. This idea is like that of sleep of which we speak to a certain extent in a state of wakefulness, but of which we have knowledge and perception only by sleep itself. Indeed, like is known only by like, and the condition of any knowledge is that the subject becomes like unto the object." I repeat, it is most difficult to understand this without preparation; and I believe, in spite of our preparatory studies, that most of this mysticism will seem to us purely theoretical, and that most of these experiences of supernatural psychology are of appeal to us only in the character of spectators.

The philosophic imagination is a very slow and dull faculty of education. We are there, suddenly, at the outposts of human thought, and well beyond the polar circle of the mind. It is strangely cold there; it is extraordinarily sombre; yet you will find there nothing save flames and light. But to those who come there, without having accustomed their soul to the new perceptions, this light and these flames are as obscure and as icy as though they were painted. The most exact of sciences is at stake here; the question is in looking over the most rugged and the most inhabitable capes of the divine "Know Thyself," and the sun of midnight reigns upon the swelling sea, where the psychology of man blends itself with the psychology of God.

It is ever of importance to remember this; you are concerned here with a very profound science, and not with a dream. Dreams are not for every one; dreams have no roots, while the incandescent flower of divine metaphysics blooms here and has its roots in Persia, India, Egypt and Greece. And yet it [science] seems as unconscious as a flower, and is ignorant of its sources.

On Emerson and Other Essays

Unhappily it is well-nigh impossible for us
to put ourselves in place of the soul, which,
without effort, conceived this science; we
can neither perceive it *ab intra* nor reproduce it in ourselves. It lacks for us what
Emerson also would call "central spon-
taneity." We can no longer change these
ideas into our own substance; and, at the
most from without, we can only take account of the prodigious experiences which
are within range of only a very few souls
during the existence of a planetary system.

"It is not legitimate," writes Plotinus,
"for us to enquire whence this intuitive
science springs, as if it were something de-
pendent on place and motion; for it does
not come from here, nor does it start out
from there in order to go elsewhere; but
it either appears or does not appear. So
that we need not pursue it with the inten-
tion of discovering in it any secret sources;
but we must wait in silence until it dazzles

suddenly upon us, in preparing us for the sacred spectacle, as the eye waits patiently for the rising of the sun."

And elsewhere he adds: "It is not by imagination or by reasoning, obliged to derive its principles from elsewhere, that we picture to ourselves comprehensible things (that is to say what is there above), but by the faculty we possess of contemplating them, the faculty which allows us to speak of them in this world. We see them awakening in us here the same power we should awaken in ourselves when we are in the intelligible world. We resemble the man who, climbing the summit of a peak, would perceive invisible objects with his own eyes for those who have not climbed with him."

But though everything, from the stone and the plant up to man, be contemplations, they are unconscious contemplations, and it is very difficult for us to treasure in

ourselves some memory of the former activity of the dead faculty. We are in this
respect similar to the eye in the neo-platonic
image: "It moves away from the light so
as to see the shadows; but because of that
very fact it does not see. For it cannot see
shadows within the light, yet without light
it does not see. In this way, while not seeing, it sees the shadows as far as it is natu-
rally capable of seeing them."

I know what opinion most men will have
of this book. They will consider it the
work of a deluded monk, of a wild solitary
man, of a recluse, delirious with fast, and
consumed by fever. They will see in it an
extravagant and dark dream crossed with
immense flashes, and nothing more. This
is the ordinary idea we have of mystics, and
people too often forget that all certainty is
in them alone. After all, if it be true, as
it has been said, that every man is a
Shakespeare in his dreams, then we should

ask if every man in his life is not a silent
mystic, a thousand times more transcendental than those who have limited themselves
by words? What is the action of the man
whose last motive is not mystic? And is
not the eye of the lover, or of the mother a
thousand times more abstruse, more im-
penetrable, and more mystic than this book,
poor and explainable after all, like all
books which are nought but dead mysteries
whose horizon no longer changes? If we
do not comprehend this, it is probably because we no longer understand anything.

But to return to our author, some will
readily recognise that, far from being
driven mad by hunger, solitude, and fever,
this monk on the contrary possessed one of
the wisest, one of the most exact, and one
of the most philosophical minds that has
ever existed. He lived, we are told, in his
hut at Groenendael amidst the forest of
Soignes. This was at the beginning of one

of the most savage centuries of the middle
ages: the fourteenth. He did not know
Greek, nor, probably, Latin. He was alone
and poor. Yet, in the depths of this obscure Brabantine forest, his soul, ignorant
and simple, received without knowing it,
the dazzling reflections of all the solitary
and mysterious summits of human thought.
He knew, unconsciously, the Platonism of
the Greeks, the Sufism of Persia, the
Brahmanism of India, and the Buddhism of
Thibet, and his wonderful ignorance resur-
rected the wisdom of buried centuries, and
foresaw the science of centuries yet to be
born. I could quote whole pages from
Plato, Plotinus, Porphyry, the Zendic
books, the Gnostics, and the Kabbala whose
almost divine substance is found intact in
the writings of this humble Flemish priest.*

* I will give only an elementary example of it in
two senses of the word. Ruysbroeck distinguishes
three kinds of life: the active life, the inner life,
and the superessential life. The Gnostics distinguish the spirit, the soul, and the material life,

On Emerson and Other Essays

There are here many strange coincidences and many disquieting agreements.
What is more, at moments he seems to have
fathomed accurately most of his unknown
predecessors; and just as Plotinus begins his
austere journey at the cross-roads where
Plato, frightened, comes to a standstill and
kneels, so we might say that Ruysbroeck
has awakened, after a slumber of several
centuries, not that kind of thought (for
that kind of thought never sleeps), but that
kind of speech which was asleep upon the
mountains where Plotinus, dazzled, had
forsaken it by placing his hands over his
eyes, as before an immense fire.

and divide men into three classes: the pneumatics
or spirituals; the psychics or animals; and the hyli-
ques or materials. Plotinus likewise separates in
the soul: intelligence, the reasonable soul, and ani-
mal nature. The Zohar notes the spirit, the soul,
and the life of the senses; and in the two systems,
as in Ruysbroeck, the connection of the three principles is explained by a *procession* assimilated with
an irradiation; then the theory of the divine encounter: God coming in us from the inside toward
the outside; we, going to him, from the outside
toward the inside, etc. Read also the 5th Ennead.,
etc., etc.

But the organism of their thought differs singularly. Plato and Plotinus are above all, princes of dialectic. They reach mysticism through the science of reasoning. They make use of their discursive soul, and seem to mistrust their intuitive or contemplative soul. Reasoning contemplates itself in the mirror of reasoning, and forces itself to dwell indifferent to the intrusion of all other reflections. It continues its course as a river of fresh water in the midst of the sea, with the presentiment of approaching absorption. Here, on the contrary, we meet again the habits of Asiatic thought; the intuitive soul reigns supreme above the discursive purification of ideas by words.

The shackles of the dream have fallen. Is it less sure? None can say. The mirror of human intelligence is entirely unknown in this book; but there exists another mirror, more sombre and more profound, which we harbour in the innermost depths of

our being; no detail can be seen there distinctly, nor can words remain on the surface; intelligence would shatter it [the mir-
ror], if for an instant it reflected there its
profane light; but something else shows itself there at times: Is it the soul? Is it
God Himself? or both at the same time?
One will never know. And yet these almost
invisible apparitions are the unique and effective sovereigns in the life of the most in-
credulous and of the blindest amongst us.
Here you will perceive nothing more than
glittering reflections in this mirror, and as
its treasure is inexhaustible, these reflections
will not resemble any of those that we have
experienced within ourselves; and despite
everything, their certitude will appear extraordinary. And that is why I know nothing more appalling than this sincere book.
In the world there is not a psychological
notion, a metaphysical experience, a mystical
intuition, however abstruse, however pro-

found, and however unforeseen they may be, that it would not be possible for us, were it necessary, to reproduce or to revive an instant within ourselves, in order to assure us of their human identity. But here we are like unto the blind father no longer able to recall the look of his children. None of these thoughts has the filial or brotherly aspect of an earthly thought; we seem to have lost the experience of God, and yet all affirms to us that we have not entered into the house of dreams. Must we exclaim with Novalis that the time is no more when the spirit of God was comprehensible, and that the meaning of the world is forever lost? That formerly all was apparition of the Spirit, but that now we observe only some dead reflections that we no longer understand, and that we live only on the fruits of better times?

I think we must declare humbly that the key to this book is not to be found along

134

the ordinary paths of the human spirit.
This key is not destined for worldly gates,
and we must be worthy of it by going as
far as possible from earth. Only one guide
is still met in these solitary crossroads, and
he can give us the final directions toward
these mysterious Icelands of fire, and these
Icelands of abstraction and of love. Plotinus it is who makes an effort to analyse,
by means of human intelligence, the divine
faculty which prevails here. He has felt
what we call by a word which explains nothing, the same ecstasies, which in reality are
only the beginning of the complete discovery of our being; and amidst their troubles
and their darkness, he has not for an instant closed the questioning eye of the psy-
chologist who seeks to render an account of
some of the most unusual phenomena of his
soul. He is thus the last pier whence we
can discern, however slightly, the waves and
the horizon of this obscure sea. He makes

an effort to extend the paths of ordinary intelligence to the heart of these devastations, and that is why we must return there unceasingly; for he is the only analytical mystic. To those who attempt these amazing excursions, I wish to give here one of the pages wherein he has attempted to explain the organism of this divine faculty of introspection.

"In intellectual intuition," he says, "the intellect sees intelligible objects by means of the light which the Supreme Source sheds over them, and in seeing these objects, it really sees the same intelligible light. But as it gives its attention to illumined objects, it does not see very clearly the principle that illumines them; if, on the contrary, it neglects the objects it sees so as to contemplate only the light which renders them visible, it sees the light itself and the principle of light. But it is not outside of itself that intelligence contemplates intelligible light

On Emerson and Other Essays

[or the light which makes the object intelligible. In Catholic doctrine, the principle
of intellection.]. It resembles then the eye
which, without considering an exterior and
strange light, before even perceiving it, is
suddenly struck by a splendour which is its
own, or by a ray which springs forth from
itself and appears to it amidst darkness. It
is the same when the eye, so as to see no
other objects, closes its lids and draws from
itself its own light, or when, pressed by the
hand, it perceives the light which it has
within itself. Then, without seeing anything on the outside, it sees; it sees even
more than at other moments, for it sees the
light [by which it sees]. The other objects
that it saw previously, while luminous, were
not the light itself. Likewise, when intelligence closes its eye in some way to other
objects, when it concentrates within itself,
seeing nothing, it sees not an unknown light
which shines in strange forms, but its own

light which suddenly shines inwardly with a pure brightness."*

"It is necessary," he tells us again, "that the soul which studies God should form an idea of Him while seeking to know Him; it is furthermore necessary that, knowing to what great things it desires to unite itself, and persuaded that it will find bliss in this union, it should steep itself in the depths of divinity, until, instead of contemplating itself, of contemplating the intelligible world, it becomes itself an object of contemplation, and shines with a splendour of conceptions which have their source above."

This is nearly all that human wisdom can tell us here on earth; it is nearly all that the prince of transcendental metaphysics has been able to express. As for the other explanations, we must find them in ourselves, within the depths where all explana-

*Plotinus, 5th Ennead. Book V. (Translation by M. N. Bouillet.)

tion is annihilated in its expression. For this is not alone in heaven or on earth; it is above all within ourselves that there are more things than all our philosophers can contain,* and since we are no longer obliged to formulate what is mysterious in us, we are more profound than all that has been written, and we are greater than all that exists.

Now, if I have translated this book, it is solely because I believe that the writings of the mystics are the purest diamonds of the wondrous treasure of humanity; though a translation may be useless probably, for experience seems to prove that it matters little whether the mystery of the incarnation of a thought take place in light or in shadow; it suffices that it has taken place. But however that may be, mystic truths have a strange license over ordinary truths; they can neither grow old nor die. There is no

*Cf. "Hamlet," Act i, Scene V.

truth which could not, one morning, descend upon this world, admirable in power, in youth, and covered with fresh and wonderful dew appropriate to things which have not yet been said. Go to-day through the infirmaries of the human soul where people come to die every day, you will never find there any mystic thoughts. They have the immunity of the angels of Swedenborg which hasten continually toward the springtime of their youth, so that the oldest angels seem the youngest; and yet, whether they come from India, Greece, or the North, they have neither country nor anniversary, and wherever we encounter them they seem immovable and real, like God Himself.

A work only grows old in proportion to its anti-mysticism; and that is why this book bears no date. I know that it is abnormally confusing; but I believe that a sincere and candid author is never obscure in the ever-

lasting sense of the word, for he always un-
derstands himself, and infinitely beyond
what he says. Artificial ideas alone arise
from actual shadows, and flourish only in
literary epochs, and in the bad faith of too
conscious centuries, when the thought of the
writer remained on this side of what he expressed. There, it was the fruitful shade of
a forest, and here, it is the obscurity of a
vault wherein are born sombre parasites.
We must also take count of this unknown
world which his phrases were to enlighten
through the double and poor medium of
words and of thoughts. Words, as some
one has said of them, were invented for
the ordinary uses of life, and they are un-
lucky, restless and amazed, like vagabonds
around a throne, when from time to time
some royal soul leads them elsewhere. And
on the other hand is thought ever the exact
image of the unfathomable which prompted
it, and is it not always the shadow of a

On Emerson and Other Essays

struggle which we see in it, like that of
Jacob with the angel, and confused in proportion with the size of the soul and of the
angel?

Woe unto us, says Carlyle, if we have in
us only what we are able to express and to
show! I know that in these pages there are
the reflected shadow of objects we do not recall having seen, whose use the monk does
not stop to explain, and which we will only
recognise when we see the objects themselves on the other side of life; but, meanwhile, which forced us to look further, and
that is much. I know again that many of
his phrases float almost like transparent
icicles on the colourless sea of silence, but
they exist; they have been separated from
water, and that is enough. I know, finally,
that the strange plants he has cultivated on
the summits of the spirit are surrounded by
spacious clouds, but these clouds offend only
those who look at them from below, and

should one have the courage to climb, one would find that they are the very atmosphere itself of these plants, and the only one wherein they can bloom, sheltered by inexistence.

For it is a vegetation so subtle that it is scarcely discernible from the silence where it has drawn its sap and where it seems inclined to dissolve itself. This whole work, besides, is like a magnifying glass, applied to shadow and to silence; and sometimes one does not see immediately the end of the ideas that still are steeped in it. It is something invisible, which at moments appears, and some attention is evidently necessary to watch its returns. This book is not too remote from us; it is probably at the very centre of our humanity. But it is we who are too far from this book; and if it seems to us disheartening like the desert, if the desolation of divine love seems terrible there, and thirst at the summits unbearable, it is not the work which is too ancient, but we who are too old perhaps, and sad and without courage, like some old men around a child. And it is another mystic, Plotinus, the great pagan mystic, who probably has the upper hand over us, when he says to those who complained of having seen nothing on the heights of introspection:

"It is at first necessary to make the organ of vision analogous to and similar to the object which it is to contemplate. Never would the eye have perceived the sun had it not first taken the form of the sun; in the same way, never would the soul have seen beauty if at first it had not become beautiful itself, and every man should begin by making himself beautiful and divine so as to obtain the view of beauty and of divinity."

II

The life of Jean van Ruysbroeck, like that of the majority of great thinkers of this world, is entirely within himself; and he himself said: "I have nothing to do with the outside." Nearly all of his biographers, Surius among others, have written almost two centuries after his death, and their work appears rather legendary. We see therein a hermit saint, silent, ignorant, extraordinarily humble, extraordinarily good, and living, unknown to himself, in the practice of miracles. The trees, under which he went to pray to God, were illuminated with an aureole; the bells of a Dutch convent rang of their own accord on the day of his death, and his body, exhumed five years after the abandonment of his soul, was found intact, amidst wonderful exhalations of perfumes which healed the sick brought from neighboring villages.

Here in a few lines are the things his-
torically certain: He was born the year
1274 at Ruysbroeck, a small village between Hal and Brussels. He was at first
vicar in the church of Sainte-Gudule; then
by the counsel of the hermit, Lambert, he
left the Brabantine village and retired to
Groenendael (the Green Valley) within the
forest of Soignes, in the vicinity of Brussels.
Some holy companions soon joined him
there, and with them he founded the abbey
of Groenendael, whose ruins are still visible
to-day. It was in this retreat that, attracted by the strange renown of his theosophy and of his superhuman visions, some
pilgrims, the Dominican Jean Tauler and
Gerard the Great, among many others,
came from Germany and from Holland to
visit the humble old man, and returned
therefrom full of an admiration of which
they have left remembrance in their works.

He died, according to the *Necrologium*

On Emerson and Other Essays

Monasterii viridis vallis, on December 2, 1381, and those of his time surnamed him the Admirable.

At that time it was the century of mystics and the period of sinister wars in Brabant and in Flanders; of violent nights of blood and of prayers under the fierce reigns of the three Johns, and of long battles even within this forest where the saints knelt. Saint Bonaventure and Saint Thomas Aquinas had just died, and Thomas à Kempis used to go and study God in this mirror of the absolute which the visionary Flemish had abandoned in the remotest part of the Green Valley, while after John of Bruges, the Van Eycks, Roger van der Weyden, Hugh van der Goes, Thierry Bouts and Hans Memlinck were to populate with images the desert word of the hermit.

Here is a catalogue of Ruysbroeck's writings; his work was enormous. There are: "The Book of the Twelve Béguins,"

"The Mirror of Eternal Salvation," "The Book of the Spiritual Tabernacle," "The Glittering Stone," "The Book of Supreme Truth," "The Book of the Seven Degrees of Spiritual Love," "The Book of the Seven Chateaux," "The Book of the Kingdom of the Loved Ones," "The Book of the Four Temptations," "The Book of the Twelve Virtues," "The Book of the Christian Faith," and "The Ornament of Spiritual Marriages," and, in addition, seven letters, two canticles, and a prayer, under the title in Surius: *Epistolæ septem utiles, Cantiones duæ admodum spiritales* and *Oratio perbrevis sed pia valde*, of which I have not been able to recover the original texts in any of the Flemish manuscripts.

Most of these writings were edited with the greatest care, a few years ago, by a society of Flemish bibliophiles: *De Maetschappij der Vlaemsche Bibliophilen;* and it is upon the excellent text of this edition that the major part of this translation has been based.

I will not here undertake an analysis of these diverse works; that analysis would be difficult, monotonous, and useless. Every book by our author treats exclusively of the same science; a theosophy appropriate to Ruysbroeck, the minute study of the soul's introversion and introspection, the contemplation of God above images and similes, and the drama of divine love on the uninhabitable summits of the spirit. I will be satisfied, therefore, to give a few characteristic extracts from each of these books.

The "Book of the Twelve Béguins," in the Latin translation by Surius, is entitled: *De vera contemplatione, opus præclarum, variis divinis institutionibus, eo quo Spiritus sanctus suggessit ordine descriptis, exuberans.* That more exactly describes the work, but it is found in none of the original manuscripts. To tell the truth, according

to the custom of his times, Ruysbroeck
rarely named his writings; and the titles
which individualise them apparently have
been interpolated by the copyists, like the
marginal rubrics of the chapters. In the
edition of the *Maetschappy der Vlaemsche
bibliophilen* are gathered together under the
title *Dat boec van den twaelf beghinen:*
first, this treatise of the contemplative life of
which Surius speaks, then a kind of manual
of symbolic astrology, and finally some reflections upon the passion and the death of
our Lord Jesus Christ. The three works
are moreover clearly separated, and Ruysbroeck plainly indicates the place where he
renounces the inner universe in order to
descend toward the visible heaven, when he
declares, at the close of Chapter XXXI:
"And after this, I abandon the contemplative life, which is God Himself and which
He grants to those who have renounced to
themselves and who have followed His

spirit there where He enjoys Himself with His Disciples, in eternal glory."

The first eight chapters of this book are written in odd and very beautiful verse, where there constantly pass ardent spiritual flashes across similes, as through the windows of a cloister that has been burned, and also benumbed sadnesses somewhat similar to Villon or Verlaine, on the dark background of essential love.

Here are some of these verses:

"Contemplation is a science without form,*
Which ever remains above reason.
It is not able to descend into reason,
And reason cannot rise above to it.
The absence of illumined form is a beautiful mirror

*The French *mode* has its English equivalent, with a double meaning. Psychologically, it is defined as "a faculty or a phenomenon of mind considered as a state of consciousness." In the philosophical or physical science sense, it means, "the manner of the existence of a thing, so far as it is not essential."

Wherein gleams the eternal splendour of
    God.
The absence of form is without manner,
And all the works of reason fail there.
The absence of form is not God,
But it is the light which makes us see.
Those who move in the absence of form,
Within divine light,
See in themselves a largeness.
The absence of form is above reason,
But not without reason.
It sees everything without astonishment.
Astonishment is beneath it;
The contemplative life is without astonish-
    ment.
The absence of form sees, but it knows not
    what;
It is above everything, and it is neither this
    nor that."

Then, the poet, recognising that his
verses were too much wrapped in darkness,

in their approach toward eternal knowledge, tells us suddenly and very simply:

"At present I must cease to rhyme,
So as to speak clearly of contemplation."

From then, he makes use of a strange prose, obscure as the terrible void which he discerns, analogous to the great cold which exists above images, with bluish jets through the obscure coldness of abstraction. And when he descends a moment to similes, he touches only the most distant, the most subtle, and the most unknown; he thus loves mirrors, reflections, the crystal, fountains, glittering glasses, water plants, precious stones, red-hot irons, hunger, thirst, fire, fish, the stars and everything that aids him in endowing his ideas with visible forms and prostrated before love, on the transparent summits of the soul, and in fixing the unheard-of which he reveals with calm.

It is besides useless to say more, since

presently you yourself will reach the
threshold of these spiritual marriages and
will thence give heed to the motionless tempest of joy, up to the external heart of God.
Alone, in fine, he has almost fathomed
thought after death, and has shown a background of its vegetation to come amidst the
unintelligible effluence of the Holy Trinity.
I believe that this is a work which we shall
remember elsewhere, perhaps, and always.
You will see, likewise, that the most amazing effusions of Saint Thérèse are already
no longer distinguished from the height of
colourless glaciers, without air and without
light, where we shall ascend with him "beyond astonishment and emotion, above
reason and virtues," in the obscure sym-
phony of contemplation. Here is a passage
from this book:

"De altero veræ contemplationis modo.

"After that comes another form of contemplation.

"Those who are raised in the simple purity of their spirit by love and respect which they bear to God, stand in His presence the naked and uncovered vision. And from the splendour of the Father radiates a simple light, on the apparition of the bare and imageless thought, raised above senses and images, above reason and without reason, into the exalted purity of the spirit.

"This light is not God, but an intermediary between showy thought and God; it is called the light of God or the spirit of the Father. In it, God manifests Himself simply, not according to the distinction and the mode of His persons, but in the nakedness of His nature and of His substance; and in it also, speaks the spirit of the Father in the elevated thought, bare and without images. 'Contemplate me as I contemplate you.' At the same time spread the ingenuousness of simple eyes, under the shedding of the simple splendour of the Father, and they perceive the splendour of the Father, that is to say, the substance or the nature of God in simple vision, above reason and without distinction.

"This splendour and this apparition of God give to the contemplator spirit a real science of the vision of God, such as can be seen in this mortal state. In order that you may understand me well, I wish to give you a sensible image of it. When you find yourself in the dazzling radiance of the sun, and when you remove your eyes from all colour, from all attention, from all distinction, and from everything lighted by the sun, if then you follow simply with your eyes the light and the rays which radiate from the sun, you will be led into the very essence of the sun, and, similarly, if you follow the dazzling rays which flow from the splendour of God, in your simple vision, you will be led into the source of your creation, and

156

there you will find nought but· God
alone."

I now approach the second of the works
heretofore enumerated: "The Mirror of
Eternal Salvation" (*Die spieghel der Ewig-
her salicheit*) is, like all mystic writings, a
study of the joys of *introversion,* or of the
return of man unto himself, so as to be in
touch with God; forwarded by the admirable doctor, and the excellent contemplator
of the Green Valley, "To dear Sister Marguerite Van Meerbeke of the convent of
Clarisses in Brussels, the year of Our Lord
1356." In certain manuscripts the piece is
called "The Book of Sacraments," and it is
indeed the poem of Eucharistic love, above
human kind and material things, and amidst
blind emanations from God, where the soul
seems to throw off the pollen of its essence
in an eternal prevision. It requires, in order
to realise slightly, here as elsewhere, these

terrors of love, a tongue which might possess the intrinsic omnipotence of tongues almost immemorial. Now, Flemish possesses
this omnipotence, and probably several
Flemish words still have in them images of
the glacial epochs. He [Ruysbroeck],
therefore, had at his service one of the almost primitive forms of speech, wherein
words are really lamps behind ideas, while
with us, ideas must explain the meaning of
words. Also I am inclined to believe that
every language always thinks more than
man, even than the man of genius who
employs it and who is only the momentary
heart of it; and that it is thanks to the latter tongue, that a mysterious, ignorant person like Ruysbroeck has been able, by gath-
ering together his forces scattered in the
prayers after so many centuries, to write
books which scarcely suit our apprehension
to-day. I translate from this book the following fragment:

"See, here our reason and all clear actions must yield; for our powers become simple in love, and remain silent, and bend before the apparition of the Father; for the manifestation of the Father lifts the soul above reason, in bareness without images; there, the soul is simple, pure, and empty of everything, and in this pure emptiness, the Father shows His divine splendour. In this splendour, neither reason nor judgment, neither observation nor distinction, can enter; all this should remain below it, for this limitless splendour blinds the spiritual eyes, in a way that they have to flutter before the inconceivable light. But the simple eye, above reason, and at the heart of intelligence, is always open, and sees and contemplates with a naked vision, this light by that very light. Yonder there is eye against eye, mirror against mirror, image against image.

"By these three things are we like unto

God, and united to Him. For this vision in our simple eye is a living mirror that God has made in His image. His image is His divine splendour; from it He has super-abundantly filled the mirror of our soul, so that no other splendour and no other image can enter. But this splendour is not an intermediary between God and ourselves, for it is that same splendour which we see, and also the light by which we see, but not our eye which sees.

"For though the image of God be without intermediary in the mirror of our soul, and though it be united to it, this image is not, however, this mirror, for God does not become a creature. But the union of the image in the mirror is so great and so noble that the soul is called the mirror of God.

"Then, this same image of God we have received, which we carry in our soul, is the Son of God, and the eternal mirror of

On Emerson and Other Essays

God's wisdom, in which we see everything and are ourselves everlastingly reflected. However, we are not the wisdom of God; otherwise we would be able to make ourselves, which is impossible and an heretical proposition. For all that we are and all that we have we hold from God and not from ourselves. And though this sublimity be immense for our soul, it is none the less hidden to the sinner and also to many of those who are just. All that we can know in the light of nature is incomplete, without flavour and without emotion; for we cannot contemplate God or find His influence in our soul, without His aid and mercy, and without our genuine training in His love."

The "Book of the Spiritual Tabernacle" (*Dat boec van den Gheesteleken Taberna-cule*). *In Tabernaculum Mosis, et ad id pertinentia commentaria, ubi multa etiam*

On Emerson and Other Essays

Exodi, Levitici, Numerorum mysteria, divino spiritu explicantur, writes Surius, the longest work of the recluse, is the strange, naïve, and arbitrary interpretation of symbols in the ark of the Covenant and of sacrifices in the ancient law. I will give most generous extracts from this, for it shows an interesting and kindly aspect of his Flemish soul; and the application and subtlety of the artist which he employs to illuminate his symbols, just as his amusing and simple complaisance in certain effects of colour and of likeness reminds us at times of his wonderful contemporaries of the school of Cologne,—the old dream painters, Master William and Lochner, and the admirable band of unknown dreamers, who established far from him the almost supernatural reflections of spiritual beatitudes of this century and of the century following, which passed away so near to God and so far from earth.

Here is what he says *apropos* of the offering of the poor in the Jewish law:

"And they (the doves) shall hold themselves near rivers and beside fresh waters, so that should some bird come from on high, which might seize them or do them ill, they might recognise it by its reflection in the water, and guard themselves against it. The fresh water is the Holy Scripture, the life of Saints and the mercy of God. We shall see ourselves in them when we are tempted; and thus nothing will be able to harm us. These doves are of an ardent nature, and from them are often born young doves, for each time that, in the glory of God and for our bliss, we consider sin with hate and contempt, and virtue with love, we bring young doves into the world, that is to say, new virtues."

Here he pictures, by the aid of these same doves, the offering of St. Paul:

On Emerson and Other Essays

"And our Father replied that his grace
should suffice him, for virtue is fulfilled in
the malady of temptations. When he understood that, he offered these two doves
into the hands of our Lord. For he for-
sook himself and became voluntarily poor
and bent the neck of his doves (which were
his desires) under the hands of our Lord
Jesus Christ and of the Holy Church. And
Christ broke the neck and the wings of the
doves, and then he became powerless to desire, or to soar in ways other than what God
desired. And then Christ placed the head
(that is to say dead will in impotency) under the broken wings, and then the dove
was ready to be sacrificed, and then the holy
Apostle said: 'Gladly, therefore, will I
glory in my infirmities, that the power of
Christ may dwell in me.' "

Listen as well to this extraordinary explanation of the spiritual flowers embroid-
ered on the hangings of the tabernacle:

On Emerson and Other Essays

"On these four curtains of different
colours, our Lord ordered Bezaleel and
Aholiab to weave and to embroider thereon,
by needle, many ornaments. Even so, our
submissive will and our intelligence place
upon these four colours diverse ornaments
of virtues. Upon the colour white of innocence, we shall place red roses, by resist-
ing forever all that is evil. We thus preserve purity and we mortify our nature; and
there are red roses with sweet perfume
which are very beautiful on this white
colour. Again we shall embroider on innocence some sunflowers, by which we mean
obedience; for, when the sun rises in the
east, the sunflower expands toward its rays
and turns itself ever eagerly toward the
heat of the sun till its setting in the west.
And at night it closes up and hides its
colours, and awaits the return of the sun.
Even so, we will open our heart, through
obedience, toward the light of God's grace;

and humbly and eagerly we will follow
God's grace, so long as we feel the heat of
love. And when the light of grace stays its
fresh emotions, and when we feel a little or
no longer feel the heat of love, then it is the
night wherein we shut close our heart to all
that can tempt it; and thus we shall enclose
within us the golden colour of love; and
we shall await a new rising of the sun with
new splendours and with new emotions.
And in this fashion we are able to preserve
innocence ever in its splendour.

"Upon the colour of hyacinth, like unto
the air, we shall embroider birds with diverse plumage; that is to say, we shall bear
in our minds, with a clear observation, the
life and the works of saints, which are
various. And these are their diverse plumage, which are graceful and very admirable, and it is with these plumes that they
have adorned themselves and soared to the
life eternal. There are birds that we must

remark seriously; if we wish to resemble them in their plumage, we must follow them to their eternal rest. Upon the colour purple, that is to say violet or blood red, which signifies generosity, we shall place water-lilies; and they symbolise a free possession of all the treasures of God. For we notice four things about the water-lily. It keeps itself ever above water and has four green leaves between the air and the water, and it is constantly in the earth, and above is spread open to the sun; and it is a remedy to those who are too ardent. And even so, we can, through generosity and freedom of spirit, possess the streams of all the richness of God. And between this free possession of our spirit and the floods of prodigal gifts from God, we shall have green leaves; that is to say, a lofty consideration of the manner in which the liberality of God flows ever with new gifts, and in what manner the gifts flow ever

generously, according to the form of the
loved one who receives them; and in what
manner the chief cause of all gifts is the
noble background of divine love, and the
nearest cause, the wise and generous nature
of creatures, which can make them like unto
God. For none can know the wealth of
God's gifts, excepting the wise and generous man who, out of the treasures of God
can give wisely and generously to all
creatures. Let us therefore adorn generosity, and then we will be strengthened in
the land of all gifts, that is to say in the
Holy Spirit, as the water-lily is made firm
in the depths of the water. And we will
expand our heart, above all, to truth and
toward the sun of justice. And thus we are
a remedy to the whole world; for the
generous heart that possesses the treasures
of God must fill up, console, refresh,
and cool all those who are afflicted.
And it is through that that the pur-

ple colour is set in the red colour,
that is to say, in burning love. There we
will place bright stars, that is to say,
some pious and devout prayer for the good
of our neighbour, and some reverent and
hidden observance between God and ourselves. There are the stars which illumine
with their splendour the kingdom of the
heavens and of the earth, and they render
us luminous and fruitful inwardly, and
establish us in the firmament of eternal
life."

After this, I translate entirely the "Chapter on Fishes" with its astonishing similes.

"And this is why the law ordered the
Jews to eat pure fish having scales and fins,
and all the other fish were impure to them
and forbidden by law. From that we understand that our inner life must have a
vestment of virtue, and our inner being

must be covered over with reasonable consideration, in the same way that the fish is
covered and ornamented with its scales.
And our loving force must be able to move
in four ways. That is to say, by triumphing
over our own will, by loving God, by de-
siring to resist nature and to acquire virtues.
These are four fins with which our inner life
should swim, like unto fishes, in the water
of divine grace. The fish has still, in the
middle, a dorsal fin which remains motionless during all its movements. And that is
why our inner feeling, straight in the
middle, must be empty of everything and
without personal preference; that is to say,
we must allow God to act in us, and in all
things of heaven and earth.

"And there is the fourth fin which bal-
ances us in the mercy of God, and in true
divine peace. And thus our inner activity
has fins and scales, and becomes for us a
pure food which pleases God. But the

scales which clad and adorn our being should be of four colours, for certain fish have grey scales, others red scales, others green scales and still others white scales. The grey scales tell us that we must clothe our inner life with humble images, that is to say, we must think of our sins, of our lack of virtue, of the humility of our Lord Jesus Christ and of His mother, and of all things which could humble us and humiliate us, and we should love poverty and contempt as being unknown to every one and as being disdained by every one. It is the grey colour which is very beautiful in the eyes of God.

"Finally we must clad our inner life with red scales; that is to say, we must remember that the Son of God was martyred through love for us; and we must bear His Passion in memory, like unto a glorious mirror before our inner eye, so as to remind us of His love and to delight us in every sorrow. And

we will also remember the many torments
of the martyrs, who, by their sufferings, followed Christ up to and into eternal life.
There are red scales well arranged, and
they clothe agreeably our inner emotion.

"We must again ornament our inner
being with green scales. That is to say, we
must meditate attentively upon the noble life
of the confessors and of the saints—in what
fashion they despised the world, and by
what marvellous works and in what diverse
ways they honoured God and served Him.
There is the colour green which attracts and
delights the amorous heart and the sound
eye. This is why, let us stir our fins, and
follow the saints by means of all the good
works possible.

"After that, we must array our inner
being in white scales; that is to say, we must
look at ourselves with the purity of virgins,
and observe in what fashion they fought
and vanquished flesh and blood, that is the

tendency of nature [natural inclination]. And that is why they carry the crown of gold and follow the lamb, that is to say Christ, with new songs which none will chant except those who have preserved chastity of soul and body. But if we have lost purity, we might, however, acquire innocence and clothe ourselves with other virtues, reaching the day of judgment more luminous than the sun, and possessing the glory of God eternally and without end.

"And that is why we must cover our inner being with four kinds of scales, and each kind should have the living fins of good will; that is to say, it is essential for us to wish to accomplish by works what we understand by reason. Thus, the inner nourishment is pure; for all science and all wisdom, without the virtuous life, are scales without fins; and all virtues practised without consideration are fins without scales; and that is why we must know, love, and

practise virtues so that our life may be pure;
and then we will be nourished with pure
fish which have scales and fins."

And the following passage:

"Afterwards, each lamp had a vase of
gold, full of water, wherein one used to put
out the fire taken from the lights [of the
church]. In this we must learn that each
gift requires of our spirit so simple a purpose in each cardinal virtue, that we might
experience in ourselves an amorous predilection toward the union with God. And
that is what we observe, likewise, in Jesus
Christ, who is our mirror for all things: for
in every virtue which He exercised He ex-
ceeded so lovingly that He sought with love
for union with His Father.

"And we must reunite all our predilec-
tions in this loving predilection which He
performed toward His Father in every

cardinal virtue. For these loving predilec-
tions are our golden vases, full of water,
that is to say, of truth and justice, and we
must immerse in them our burning wicks,
that is to say, the acts of all the virtues we
have practised; we must extinguish them
there, and plunge them therein, by com-
mitting ourselves to His justice, and join-
ing ourselves to His venerable merits.
Without that the wick of all our virtues
would smoke and smell badly before God
and all His saints."

Elsewhere he examines the twelve gems
of the high priest's breastplate, and observes in them reflections of eternal symbols,
as well as unforeseen, exact, and revealing
analogies. Judge of it:

"In the rays of the sun, the topaz exceeds
in splendour all precious stones; and, likewise, the humility of our Lord Jesus Christ

exceeds in splendour and sublimity all saints and angels, by reason of His union with the eternal Father. And in this union the reflection of the divine sun is so bright and so glorious, that it attracts and reflects in its splendour, in a simple vision, all the looks of saints and of angels, and those likewise of all just men to whom this splendour is revealed. And in this fashion, the topaz attracts and reflects also within itself the looks which are before it, because of its great clearness. But if you were to cut the topaz, it would become obscured, and if you were to leave it in its natural state, it would remain clear. And, likewise, if you desire to search and to fathom the splendour of the Word eternal, that splendour will be obscured and you will lose it. But leave it there as it is and follow it with a simple vision, in the abnegation of yourself, and it will enlighten you."

On Emerson and Other Essays

Now examine the strange relation seen imperfectly through other stones.

"In this article [of the Creed] we compare Christ to the noble sapphire, of which there are two kinds. The first is yellow, with purple tints, and seems mixed with golden powder; the other is sky blue, and in the reflections of the solar rays it gives forth a burning splendour, and one cannot look through it. And we find all that in our Lord, in this fifth article. For when His noble soul ascended to heaven, His body lay in the tomb, yellow, because of the flight of the soul; purple because of His bloody wounds; and mingled with golden powder, because he was joined to the divinity. And His soul descended to hell, sky blue, in such manner that His friends were rejoiced and became wondrously happy in His splendour.

"And in His resurrection, the splendour

177

became so potent and so huge in body and soul, because of the irradiation of the sun of the divinity, that it shot forth flashes and burning rays, and kindled with love all that it touched. And this noble sapphire, Christ, no one can look through, for He is without depth, according to divinity."

I pass by the amethyst, "from which seem to emanate red roses," and I close this [selection] by translating the final symbols of the chrysolite, the emerald, and the jasper.

In the first place, the chrysolite:

"This communion of saints and the remission of sins are obtained by the *waves of the night,* that is to say, by two sacraments of the Holy Church, baptism and penance. They are the waves which cleanse by faith the night of darkness: sin. And God made this oath at the time of Abraham, that He

would give Himself to us and become as
one of us; and because of His abundant
common love He wished to wash us in His
blood. And so that we might without
doubt believe in His oath which He had
sworn to Himself, He sealed it with His
own death and the rewards of His death
He gave in common to the Holy Church
for the remission of sins, and to the saints
for the ornament of their glory. This
article, 'the communion of saints and the
forgiveness of sins,' is symbolised for us by
the chrysolite; for it is like the waters of
the sea in its translucidity and in its greenness, and what is more, it has golden reflections. And, likewise, all the saints and
all the just are translucent through grace
or glory, and they are green through their
holy life, and they have golden reflections
through divine love by which they are
transillumined. And these three ornaments
are common to all saints and to all just

people, for they are the treasure of the holy churches, here and in eternal life. And all those who have through penitence put from them the colour of the red sea, that is to say a sinful life, are like unto the chrysolite.

"You know that this sea is red because of the country and of the depths in which it is; it is between Jericho and Zorah. Jericho signifies the moon and Zorah the beast that blinds reason. Between the moon of inconstancy and the inclination of reason toward the beast, resides the red sea, that is to say, an impure life. No creature can dwell alive in the red sea, and all that does not live in it goes to the bottom, and that is why it is called the dead sea, because it has no movement in it, and it is like unto bitumen or pitch, for it seizes and kills everything that comes into it, and in this way it is like unto sin which seizes man and kills him spiritually before the eyes of God, forcing him into hell."

Here, finally, the application of the
emerald and of the jasper, to the third and
to the sixth article of the Apostle's Creed:

"In this article, we compare to the Son
of God the beautiful stone which is called
emerald, and which is so green that leaves
and herbs, and everything that is green, cannot equal its greenness. And by its greenness it fills and nourishes the eyes of men
who regard it. Now, when the eternal
Word of the Father was made flesh, the
colour was the greenest that had ever been
seen. This union is so green and so fine
and so joyful, that no other colour can equal
it; and that is why it has filled and nourished the eyes of men who have prepared
themselves in a godly vision. If one should
cut and polish the emerald, there is nothing softer or more agreeable to the eye, and
we can recognise in it and observe in it
everything that is before it, as in a mirror.

And likewise, if we should detail intently
the existence of Him who adopted our
nature through love of us, we must admire,
nor can we satiate with praise, His sublimity. And when we consider how He was
made man, we should, because of His
humility, hate ourselves and be unable sufficiently to humble ourselves. And when we
examine the motive for which He was made
man, we cannot rejoice sufficiently nor can
we love Him enough.

"In these three ways we must consider
longingly, and polish and examine lovingly,
Christ, the noble emerald. In so doing, we
will find nothing so pleasing to the eyes of
our reason, nor anything that attracts them
more, for we find Him reflected in us and
we find ourselves reflected in Him through
His grace and a virtuous life, and that is
why we should turn ourselves away from
temporal things and always carry this
mirror before us.

On Emerson and Other Essays

"And, in another article, we compare Christ to the noble jasper, which is green in colour and pleasing to the eye, and it is almost like the emerald in its greenness. And that is why we liken it to the ascension of our Lord, who was green and beautiful before the eyes of the Apostles, and so pleasing, that they were never able to forget Him during all their lives. And we shall justly feel the same thing in ourselves; we consider the noble emerald, the eternal Word, as having descended into our nature, and through love for us, with a supereffluent viridity, and we shall ourselves rejoice in that above all, for this vision is full of graces. We shall consider afterwards how the glorious jasper, that is to say Jesus Christ, ascended to heaven with our nature, and, seated on the right hand of the Father, has prepared for us the state of glory. Amen."

Then comes the book of the "Twelve Virtues" that Laurentius Surius more exactly entitles *Tractatus de præcipuis quibusdam virtutibus*. The hermit of Groenendael appears to have made some violent effort to open his earthly eyes; and all his thoughts are interlaced, with the ingenuousness of divine children, in the green and blue rays of humility and mercy, while his prose, ordinarily without personalities, is here enlivened with counsels and with diverse events. Here is a fragment on humility:

"To reach the inferior place [Catholic: lowest plane] is to preserve nothing of evil; and, as we have always something to foresake, as long as we are mortal, we never attain the lowest plane, because to perish is to become, not according to the senses, but according to the negation of them.*

*Translator's note: According to Catholic doctrine, the lowest plane of humility is the highest plane of virtue; to die unto one's self is to live.

And should some one say that immersion in humility is the lowest plane, I would not combat it. But it seems to me that to immerse one's self in humility is to immerse one's self in God; for God is the foundation of humility, and He is at equal height and at equal depth above and below from every place. And between the lowering and the coming to the lowest plane, there is a difference, as far as I can see. For to attain the lowest plane is to preserve nothing of evil, and to experience the abasement is to immerse one's self in humility, and that is annihilation in God and death in God.

"Now, we always have something to give up as long as we live, and to have nothing more to give up is to have attained the lowest plane. That is why we are not able to reach the lowest plane. For what man has been so humble, that he could not have been more humble still, and who has loved so ardently, that he could not have loved more ardently still? Save Christ, certainly no one. And that is why, let us never be contented as long as we are mortal, for we can always become more humble than we are to-day. And it is fortunate that we have a Lord and a God so great that we can never render Him sufficient honour or homage.

"Yes, even if one of us could do all that all men and all angels can do at every moment. But if we immerse ourselves in humility, that is enough for us, and we satisfy God by Himself, for we are in this immersion *a life* with Him, not according to nature, but through immersion, since by humility we have lowered ourselves below our creation and we are absorbed in God, who is the foundation of humility. And there He fails us in nought, for we ourselves are immersed through ourselves in God, and there are no more gifts nor acceptances, nor anything that we might call

there, for there is neither *here* nor *there,*
but I know not *where.*"

I transcribe again, from the same book,
the passage which follows on indifference
to everything:

"Now, he who has found God ruling
thus in him, by reason of grace, and who
abides in God above the work of fortitude,
may dwell insensible to joy, to sorrow, and
to the multiplicity of creatures. For God
has penetrated him, and he is more inclined
to look within himself than to look without;
and this essence recalls itself to him everywhere man is found; and this inclination
and this essence are never forgotten, unless
man deliberately turns himself away from
God, which he will not willingly do; for he
who has tried God in this way cannot easily
turn away from God; not that this cannot
happen, for no one is certain of anything

while he is mortal, unless some revelation [takes place].

"The man that God has penetrated in this way, God takes him up divinely, and enlightens him in all things, for all things have for him a divine taste. For he who relates everything to the glory of God, has the taste of God in all things, and God is reflected for him in all things. For he takes all from God's hand, thanks Him, and praises Him in everything, and God shines and gleams, all the time, for he waits upon God with great care, and never willingly turns himself toward useless things. And when he sees that he is turned toward useless things, he turns away from them immediately with great bitterness against himself; and laments to God of his inconstancy, and determines within himself never again to turn knowingly toward useless things. For all is empty and vain where there is not the glory of God, or the good of our neighbour, or our own salvation.

"He who watches thus over himself is less and less anxious, for he often has the presence of his friend, and that rejoices him above all things. He is like one who has an intense thirst. In his thirst he not only drinks, and he can think successfully of other things than the thirst which torments him, but whatever he does and whatever he be, or whatever object he thinks upon, the image of the drink is not effaced in him as long as he suffers from thirst, and the longer the thirst the more the suffering increases in man. And it is likewise for him who loves a thing so profoundly that he tastes nothing else, for nothing else goes to his heart, except what possesses him and what he loves. Wherever he be, or with whomsoever he be, whatever he begins and whatever he does, nothing estranges from him what he loves so passionately. And in all things he finds the image of what he loves, and the greater and more powerful the love, the more is it present to him; and in that purpose he is not looking for repose and idleness, for no anxiety prevents him from having, ever present, the image of what he loves."

Let us have a glimpse also of the tract on "The Christian Faith," *De fide et judicio, tractatulus insignis,* according to Surius. It forms, in its twenty pages, a kind of catechism really magnificent, from which I extract the following fragment on the happiness of the chosen:

"We will contemplate with our inner eye the mirror of God's wisdom, where all things shine and are illumined—things which will ever exist and which can gladden us. And we will hear, with our outer ears, the melody and the sweet hymns of saints and of angels who will praise God forever.

And with our inner ear we will hear the innate Word of the Father; and in this Word we will receive all science and all truth. And the sublime odour of the Holy Spirit will pass before us, sweeter than all the balms and precious herbs that ever were, and this perfume will draw us from ourselves, toward the eternal love of God, and we shall relish the eternal excellence of God, sweeter than all honey, which will nourish us and enter our soul and our body; and we will ever be hungry and thirsty for it, and through hunger and thirst the delights and nourishment will ever reside, and ever be renewed; and this is the life eternal.

"We shall understand through love, and we shall be understood through love, and God will possess us and we shall possess Him by union. We will enjoy God, and rest ourselves, united to Him, in beatitude. And this delight without form, in this super-essential repose, is the supreme foundation of beatitude, for one is here engulfed above hunger, in satiety; hunger can no longer enter into it, for there is nought but unity there; all loving spirits will rest there in the superessential shade; and nevertheless will they sleep and wake ever in the light of glory."

Then comes the book of the "Glittering Stone." *De calculo, sive de perfectione filiorum Dei, libellus admirabilis,* adds Surius. The point in question here is that of the mysterious stone of which the Spirit says in the Apocalypse: *Et dabo illı (vincenti) calculum candidum, et in calculo nomen novum scriptum, quod nemo scit nisi qui accipi* (Apoc. 11, 17). This stone, according to the monk of the forest of Soignes, is the symbol of Christ, given to lovers alone, and like a flame reflecting the love of the Word eternal. And then, these same darknesses of love open themselves, whence emerge, in palpitating flowers per-

ceived imperfectly through the gradual ex-
pansions of contemplation, and above unusual greennesses of an unequal joy, cease-
less sobs of light. Examine this:

"And from there follows the third point,
that is to say, an activity above reason and
without form; for the unity in God which
every loving spirit has possessed in love, attracts and claims externally toward the soul
of its essence, all divine persons and all loving spirits. And those who love, prove this
attraction, more or less, according to their
love and their activities. And he who
watches for this attraction and is bound to
it can no longer fall into mortal sin. But
the contemplator, who has disowned his
being and everything, does not suffer from
repulsive force, because nothing more is left
to him, and he is empty of all; and thus he
can always enter, one and without images,
into the most intimate depths of his spirit.

There, he sees coming forth an eternal light, and in this light he establishes the everlasting existence of the unity of God. And he himself feels an eternal fire of love, which above everything desires to be one with God. And the more he observes this attraction or this exigency, the more he feels it. And the more he feels it, the more he desires to be one with God, for he wishes to pay the debt that God calls upon him to pay. This. eternal exigency of the unity of God works in the spirit an eternal incandescence of love; but, as the spirit pays its debt, without interruption, this works in him an everlasting consumption; for in the reflection of unity all spirits fail in their work, and prove nothing other than the consumption of all in the simple unity of God. This simple unity of God none can feel, nor can one possess it, if he does not hold himself before the immense splendour and before love, above reason and without forms.

On Emerson and Other Essays

In this presence, the spirit feels in him an eternal burning in love; and in this incandescence of love he finds neither beginning nor end. And he feels himself *one* with this fire of love. The spirit lives always in fire within itself, for its love is eternal. And he ever feels himself consumed in love, for he is attracted in the refection of the unity of God, where the spirit burns in love. If he observes himself, he finds a distinction and a difference between God and himself, but where he burns he is simple and has no distinction, and that is why he feels nothing but unity; for the incommensurable flame of divine love consumes and absorbs all that it has enveloped in its essence.

"And you can observe thus that the attracting unity of God is no other thing than boundless love, which draws amorously toward the inner life, in an eternal delight, the Father, the Son, and all that dwells in Him. And we want to burn and consume

ourselves in this love, eternally, for in it
abides the beatitude of all spirits. And that
is why we must all of us establish our life
over a fathomless abysm; we shall thus be
able to descend everlastingly in love, and
immerse ourselves through ourselves in the
limitless depth.

"And by this same love, we shall elevate
ourselves and exceed ourselves in the inconceivable heights. And in love without
forms, we shall wander; and it shall mislead
us in the limitless expanse of God's love.
And there within we should ebb and flow
outside of ourselves, in the unknown
voluptuousness of the divine goodness and
opulence. And this shall be the fusion and
transfusion, the eternal absorption and reab-
sorption of ourselves,* in the glory of God.
Behold, in each of these comparisons I
show to the contemplator his essence and

*Translator's note: Herein is given the idea of
absorbing and of being absorbed.

his activities. But no other can understand me, for no man can educate another
in contemplation. But when eternal truth
is revealed to the spirit, it has taught the
spirit all that is necessary."

I ought really to translate for you also
the many wonders of Chapters VI, VII
and VIII, which speak "Of the difference
between the mercenary ones and the faithful
servants of God," "Of the difference between the faithful servants and the secret
friends of God," and "Of the difference between the secret friends and the occult children of God," where verily, the anchorite
of the Green Valley seems to steep his pen
on the side of this world [in other words,
approaches earth]. But can I do so after so
much excess? Finally I ask your indul-
gence still for the following and positively
the last fragment. It is wondrously beautiful.

On Emerson and Other Essays

"Now, understand; the progression is such: in our journey toward God, we must carry our being and all our works before us, as an eternal offering to God; and in the presence of God we shall rest ourselves with all our works, and dying in love, we shall surpass all creation, till in the super-essential kingdom of God. There, we will possess God in an eternal death to ourselves. And that is why the spirit of God says in the book of the Apocalypse: 'Blessed are the dead who die in the Lord.' It is not without reason that these dead are called the happy dead, for they remain eternally dead to themselves, and immersed through themselves in the joyful unity of God. And they ever die anew in love through the attractive reflection of this very unity. Then the spirit of God says again: 'They may rest from their labours, for their works follow them.' In this way where we are born from God in

a spiritual and virtuous life, we carry our
works before us as an offering to God; but
in the absence of plans, were we to die anew
in God, in a life eternally blissful, our good
works would follow us, for they are a life
with us. In our journey toward God through
virtues, God dwells in us, but in our death
to ourselves and to all things, we dwell in
God. If we have faith, hope, and charity,
we have received God; and He dwells within us with His mercy, and He sends us
abroad as His faithful servitors, to keep His
commandments. And He recalls us home
as His mysterious friends, if we follow His
counsels. But above all things, if we would
taste God, or feel in us the eternal life,
we must, over and above reason, enter into
God through our faith; and there we must
dwell simple, idle, and without models, elevated by love in the open nakedness of our
thought. For in dying in love to all things,
in dying in ignorance and in obscurity to all

attention, we are elaborated and made over by the eternal Word which is an image of the Father. And in the passivity of our spirit, we receive the incomprehensible splendour which surrounds us and penetrates us, in the same way that the air is pierced by the splendour of the sun. And this splendour is nothing more than a limitless vision and contemplation.

"What we are we behold, and what we behold we are; for our thought, our life, and our essence are merely united to the truth which is God, and are raised with it. And that is why, in this ingenuous vision, we are a life and a spirit with God, and that is what I call a contemplative life. In binding ourselves to God through love, we choose the better part; but in regarding God thus in superessence, we possess God entirely. This contemplation is joined to an activity without shape, that is to say to an annihilating life, for just when we go from ourselves, in the shadows and in the absence of limitless forms, the simple ray of the splendour of God ever shines bright; now, we are established in this ray, and it draws us outside of ourselves, in super-essence and in the submersion of love. And this submersion of love is always accompanied and followed by a shapeless activity of love. For love cannot be passive. It seeks to enter through knowledge and taste into the immense opulence which dwells at the depths of itself, and it has an insatiable hunger. Always to receive in this impotency, is to swim against the stream. One can neither do without that nor receive it; excel himself in that, nor accept it; remain silent nor speak, for it is above reason and intelligence, and that exceeds all creatures. And that is why one cannot attain it or follow it, but we shall look within ourselves: there we feel that the spirit of God leads us and pushes us in this impatience of love;

and we shall look above us; there we feel
that the spirit of God draws us outside of
ourselves, and annihilates us in Himself,
that is to say in the superessential love with
which we are one and which we possess
more profoundly and more abundantly than
anything else.

"This possession is a simple and limitless
delectation of all good and of eternal life.
And we are engulfed in this delight above
reason and without reason, in the calm
depths of divinity which will never more be
disturbed. It is through experience alone
that we can know that this is true. For why
that is, or what it is, or in what place it is,
or how it is, neither reason nor activity can
learn, and that is why our activity which
follows remains without shape, that is to
say, without manner."

"For the fathomless good which we taste
and possess, we can neither conceive nor understand, and through our activity we can

never go from ourselves to enter it. And
that is why we are poor in ourselves and
rich in God, full of hunger and thirst in
ourselves, and satiated and drunk in God,
energetic in ourselves, and with an absolute idleness in God. And we shall dwell
thus forever. For without the activity of
love, we can never possess God. And he
who feels or believes otherwise is deceived.
And thus we live completely in God, in possessing our beatitude, and we live wholly in
ourselves in training ourselves by love
toward God. And although we should live
entirely in God and wholly in ourselves,
this is nevertheless only a single life; but it
has double and contrary sensations. For
richness and poverty, hunger, gluttony,
work and idleness—these things are absolutely contrary in themselves. None the less
it is in that, that our supreme nobility
resides, now and forever more, for
we cannot completely become God, nor

can we lose our created essence; that is impossible.

"But should we remain wholly within ourselves, separated from God, we would be unhappy and not saved, and that is why we feel ourselves completely in God and wholly within ourselves; and between these two sensations, we shall find nothing except the grace of God, and the activities of our love. For, from the height of our supreme feeling, the splendour of God shines in us; which teaches us truth, and pushes us toward all the virtues in the everlasting love of God.

"We follow this splendour unceasingly, even to the source from whence it flows; and there we feel nought else than the stripping of the spirit, and the immersion in simple and infinite love, forever. If we remain there always, by our simple vision, we should ever feel that, for our immersion in the divine reflection, dwells forever and unceasingly, provided we have departed from ourselves, and provided we possess God in the submersion of love. For if we possess God in the submersion of love, that is to say in the loss of ourselves, God is ours and we are His, and we immerse ourselves, through ourselves, in our possession which is God, forever and ever. This immersion is necessary by habitual love, and that is why it has a place during sleep and during wakefulness, whether one knows it or not.

"And in this way, this immersion does not deserve any other praises, but it keeps us in possession of God, and of all the benefits that we have received from Him. And this immersion is like unto rivers, which, ceaselessly and forever, flow always into the sea, for that is the place which is proper for them. And likewise, if we possess God alone, our essential immersion through habitual love flows forever, in an abysmal feeling which we possess and which is appropriate to us. If we were always simple, and if we always considered absolutely, we would always have a like sensation. Now, this immersion is above all virtues, and above all the practices of love. For it is nothing more than an eternal going from ourselves, by a distinct prevision, in eagerness, toward which we incline ourselves, outside of ourselves, as toward a beatitude. For we feel an eternal tendency outside of ourselves, toward another than ourselves. And that is the closest and the most occult distinction that we can see between God and ourselves; and above it there is no longer any difference. None the less, our reason remains, with open eye, in the shadow; that is to say in infinite ignorance, and in this darkness remains occult and hidden from us, the limitless splendour, for the coming of its immensity blinds our reason. But it envelops us in simplicity, and transforms us by its essence, and thus we are elaborated beyond our personality, and transformed up to the immersions of love, where we possess bliss and are one with God."

Here now is the "Book of the Seven Steps of the Ladder of Love" (called by Surius *De septem gradibus amoris, libellus optimus*), wherein the prior of Groenendael studies seven virtues, which lead from introversion to the border of absorption. I think this is one of the most beautiful of the saint's books—all of which are strange and beautiful. It would be necessary for me here to translate sufficiently some of these extraordinary passages; among others that wherein he concerns himself with four melodies of heaven, but space is lacking in this introduction, which is already too long. I will therefore be contented with transcribing the page which follows:

"The Holy Spirit speaks loudly in us

with high voice and without words: 'Love
Love Who forever loves you.' His clamour
is an inner tenderness in our spirit. This
voice is more terrible than the storm. The
flashes that He sends forth open heaven to
us, and show us light and eternal truth. The
heat of His touch and of His love is such
that He wants to consume us wholly. His
touch in our spirit cries out unceasingly:
'Pay your debt, love Love Who eternally
loves you.' From that are born a great
inner restlessness and a resignation without
shape. For the more we love, the more we
will desire to love; and the more we pay
what love demands of us, the more we dwell
debtors to Love. Love is not silent, and
He cries eternally: 'Love Love.' It is an
unknown fight with strange feelings. To
love and enjoy is to serve and suffer. God
lives in us by means of His graces. He
teaches us, He counsels us, He orders us—
love. We live in Him above grace, and

above our works, in suffering and in enjoyment. In us there dwell love, knowledge, contemplation, and possession, and above them joy. Our work is to love God; our pleasure is to undergo the entwining of Love.

"Between love and delight there is a distinction, as between God and His grace. Where we adhere through love, we are spirits, but where He strips us of our spirit and where He reforms us by His spirit, we are delight. The spirit of God breathes us toward love and toward good works; and it inspires us both in repose and in joy, and there is the life eternal; just as we breathe forth the air which is in us, and breathe in the fresh air, and it is just this which composes our mortal life in nature. And though our spirit be enraptured, and though its work fail in pleasure and in bliss, it is always renewed in grace, in charity, and in virtues. And that is why, to enter into an idle pleasure, to go forth in good works, and to dwell always joined to the spirit of God—this is what I love. Just as we open our material eyes, so do we see; and just as we close them rapidly, so do we not see; just as we die in God, we live outside of Him, and we dwell one with Him forever."

We next have the "Book of the Seven Chateaux," called by Laurentius Surius *De septem custodiis opusculum longe piissimum* and which is not without its analogies with the "Chateau of the Soul," by Saint Thérèse d'Avila, also with its seven dwellings, of which prayer is the portal. The hermit of the forest of Soignes sent this book, with the "Mirror of the Eternal Salvation," "to the holy sister Clarisse, Marguerite Van Meerbeke, of the Convent of Brussels," and that is why the counsel which he infuses into the prologue is a little touching. He showed her thus in what way she

will go to the window of the parlour;
piously, closing her eyes to the countenance
of man; and the joy of sorrow and the care
of the sick, with pale counsels of the hos-
pital. Then the seven spiritual chateaux of
Saint Claire arise, whose divine grace closes
the doors that it is no longer necessary to
open in order to see into the streets of one's
heart. Listen to what follows, ever on
love:

"And the loving soul cannot give itself
entirely to God, nor can it receive God entirely, for all that it receives, respecting
what is wanting to it, is a trifle and counts
for nought in its emotion. And that is why
it is stirred, and why it sinks in the impatience and in the fervour of love; for it
can neither do without God nor can it obtain
Him, reach His depth nor His summit, follow Him nor abandon Him. And it is there
you will find the tempest and the spiritual

plague of which I have spoken to you; for
no tongue can describe these many storms
and these agitations which are born from
two sides of love. For love makes man
sometimes ardent, sometimes cold, sometimes
daring, sometimes timid, sometimes joyful
and sometimes sad; it brings him fear, hope,
despair, tears, complaining, songs, praises,
and numberless similar things. That is
what those suffer who live in the transport
of love, and yet it is the most intimate and
the most useful life that man can live, according to his vocation.

"But where the vocation of man fails and
can go no higher, there begin the ways of
God: it is the one where man, by his sufferings, his love, and his unsatisfied desires, en-
twines himself with God, and cannot be
united: there, the spirit of our Lord comes
like a violent fire that burns, wastes away,
and engulfs everything in it; in such manner that man forgets all his activities and

forgets himself, and feels nothing else than if he was a spirit and a love in God. Here the senses and every force are silent, and they are satiated and soothed; for the fountain of goodness and of divine opulence has overflowed all, and each has received more than he could desire.

"Then comes the third condition which we attribute to our Heavenly Father: that in which He drains the memory of forms and images, and raises naked thought as far as its origin, which is Himself. There, man is strengthened in his beginning, which is God, and there he is united. And it has given him the force and freedom to work inwardly and outwardly, by means of all virtues. And he receives knowledge and intelligence in all activities according to reason. And he learns the manner of bearing the inner operation of God, and the transformation of divine forms above reason, just as has been said already. And above all the divine forms, he will understand, by the same intuition without forms, the essence of God without forms, which is an absence of forms. For one can neither express it by words, nor works, nor forms, nor signs, nor similitudes, but it shows itself spontaneously to the ingenious intuition of the imageless thought.

"But one may show upon the way signs and similitudes which prepare man to see the reign of God. And you will imagine this essence, like the incandescence of a limitless fire, where all is consumed in a calm, blazing, and immutable conflagration. And it is thus with the satisfied essential love, which is a possession of God and of all the saints, above all modes, and above all works, and all the practices of virtue. This love is a limitless calm and flood of riches and of joys, where all the saints are swallowed up in God and in a beatitude without limit. And this beatitude is wild and waste as a wilderness; for there is neither form, nor way, nor path, nor repose, nor measure, nor end, nor beginning, nor anything that one could express by words or show by words. And this is our simple beatitude to all, this divine essence, and our superessence above reason and without reason. If we want to feel it, it would be necessary for our spirit to surpass itself, above our created essence, toward this eternal center, where all our lines begin and end. And in this center these lines lose their name and all their distinction, and are united to this center, and become that very unity which the center is by itself, and yet converging lines remain always in themselves.

"Look; thus shall we ever dwell what we are in our created essence, and yet by the ascent of the spirit, we pass continually into our superessence. In it we will be above ourselves, below ourselves, beyond our breadth, beyond our length, in an eternal wandering forever."

I will be fairly silent about the tract of the "Four Temptations," where there are considered some very subtle dangers which menace the contemplator, and of which the most formidable is quietism; but outside of certain discoveries in the unknown psychology of the prayer, the work—very brief, as I have said,—offers no summit exceptionally intense to our soul.

The other tract, of nearly the same length,—that is to say a score of pages,—is entitled the "Book of the Supreme Truth," or "Samuel" according to Surius, who adds: *Qui alias de alta contemplatione dicitur, verius autem apologice quorumdam sancti hujus viri dictorum sublimium inscribi possit.* But this book is so wonderful that it would be necessary to translate it entirely. I shall not quote anything from it at present; since it is as indivisible as the essence of which it seems to illustrate the steady effusion in its unique and fearful mirror.

I then come to the "Book of the Kingdom of Lovers," the strangest and the most abstract work of the visionary of the Green Valley, in the midst of which the soul extends itself and is frightened in a spiritual and without doubt normal void, evoking for the spirit, which does not follow it there, some glass bells absolutely black, where there are no more air, nor images, nor anything which one could exactly conceive, except incessant stars around the void of all that is not eternal.

The book begins with this verse on wisdom: *Justum deduxit per vias rectas et ostendit illi regnum Dei*, and involves the three theological virtues and the seven gifts of the Holy Spirit. I translate immediately and more amply than ever.

On Emerson and Other Essays

In the first place, this on the deserts of the essence:

"The soul of man being made of nought, that God took from nowhere, man has followed nothing which is no part, and he has flowed from his *Self* in errors, through immersion in the simple essence of God, as in his own depths, and he is dead in God. To die in God is to be blissful, and each according to his merits—it is to be very different in grace and in glory. This bliss is to understand God and to be understood by God, in the joyful unity of divine persons, and to have emanated through this unity in the superessence of God. Now this unity being enjoyed in introversion, and fructifying in extroversion, the fountain of the unity flows: that is to say the Father begot the Son, the eternal truth, which is the image of the Father where He Himself shall be recognized in everything. This image is life, and the cause of all creatures, for in that image lies everything according to the divine mode; and by this image everything is done perfectly, and everything is ruled wisely on this pattern, and on account of the image everything is appropriated to its end, as far as it belongs to God to appropriate it; for each creature has received the means of acquiring its beatitude. But the rational creature is not the image of the Father, according to the effluence of its created form, for it flows in its capacity of creature, and that is why it knows and loves with measure in the light of grace or of glory. For no one possesses divine nature actively, according to the divine mode, if it be not divine persons; since no creature can work according to a measureless mode, for if he should work thus, he would be God and no creature.

"In His image, God has made creatures similar to Him, according to nature; and

those who are turned toward Him, He has
made them even more like, above nature in
the light of grace and of glory, each [of
them], according to its aptitude through the
state of its soul or through its merits. Now,
all those who feel the inner touch, and who
have illuminated reason and the impatience
of love, and to whom is shown the absence
of mode, have joyful introversion in the
superessence of God. Now, God is attached
to His essence in a happy manner, and contemplates that very essence He enjoys. According to the mode of the pleasure, the
divine light grows weaker and weaker in the
essence without mode; but in contemplation
and in the fixation of attention, the
vision cannot founder, for one shall
always contemplate what he enjoys.
Those who fail ceaselessly in the
light are those who rest themselves in
pleasures, amidst wild solitudes where God
is possessed in enjoyment; there fails the

light in repose and in the absence of mode in the sublime essence. There God is throned in Himself, and all those who possess God in grace and in glory to this degree, are the thrones and tabernacles of God, and they are dead in God in eternal rest.

"From this death, a superessential life is born, that is to say a contemplative life; and here begins the gift of intelligence. For God, in contemplating ceaselessly the very essence which He enjoys, and granting impatience where it renders alike, gives likewise repose and enjoyment, where He unites. But there where we are one with Him in essence and in immersion, there are no more gifts nor acceptances. And because He reconciles illumined reason, there where it renders alike, he gives also the limitless splendour there where he unites. This boundless splendour is the image of the Father. We are created in this image, and can be united to it in a sublimity higher than the thrones, provided we contemplate above failing, the glorious face of the Father, that is to say the sublime nature of divinity.

"Now, this limitless splendour has been given in common to all joyful spirits in grace and in glory. Thus it flows for all as the splendour of the sun, and yet those who receive it are not all equally enlightened. The sun shines more clearly through glass than through stone, and through crystal than through glass, and every precious stone burns and shows its nobility and its power and its colour by the splendour of the sun. In the same way, each is illumined at the same time in grace and in glory according to its aptitude for sublimity; but he who is more enlightened in grace, is less than he who is less enlightened in glory. Yet the light of glory is not intermediary between the soul and this limitless splendour; but our state, and the time, and the inconstancy disturb us, and that is why we acquire some merits, and those who are in glory do not acquire any.

"This sublime splendour is the ingenuous contemplation of the Father, and of all those who contemplate in enjoyment, and who regard it steadfastly, by means of an incomprehensible light, each according as he is illumined. For endless light shines without intermission in all thoughts, but the man who dwells here, in time, is often overwhelmed with images, in such fashion that he does not always contemplate actively and fixedly the superessence by means of this light. But he has possessed it virtually in receiving this gift, and he can contemplate, when he wishes it. The light by means of which one contemplates limitless beings and what one contemplates being abysmal,— this can never attain that; but fixation and contemplation dwell eternally in the absence of mode, in the joyful aspect of sublime

Majesty, where the Father, by eternal wisdom, regards fixedly the abyss of its essence in its mode."

A large part of this book of the "Kingdom of the Loved Ones" is written in singular verse. The ternary and breathlessly monotonous rhythm is almost like that of the "Stabat Mater"; only the third verse of each strophe reproduces the same rhyme through the whole work, and is ever sustained on an abstraction from whence arise the two preceding verses like twin flowers of restlessness and obscurity. One can imagine this music of the empty author of the inner dream of the virgins of Memlinck, whilst their secret senses, their countenance, and their small hands join in ecstasy; but, unhappily, a translation can never renew here this taste for shadows and for bread steeped in night; nor catch the image of this impression of obscurity illumined with tears, with ice crossed by red irons, and with oppression without horizon. That is why I will only translate one of these shadowy poems. It deals with the gift of intelligence:

"In order that this gift should illumine it,
It must surpass itself
In superessence.
   The measureless splendour,
He will perceive it there
In deep simplicity.
   The light of truth
Shall flow through him,
And he will disappear wholly in it.
   This general light
Shines upon those who are pure,
And illumines them according to their
     merits.
   Then they can regard
And contemplate, without sparing them-
     selves,

"The aspect of enjoyment.
    One will always contemplate
What one enjoys, with confidence,
Remotely in the loss of divine grace.
    The lover has gone very far.
That which causes the eyes to tend
Toward the sublime beatitude.
    Yet, it is attained;
And the lover possesses the beloved,
In the wastes of unity.
    We shall then dwell thus,
Forcing in ourselves our whole life
Toward the sublime abyss."

It is necessary to translate a few more bits from this exceptional volume. But it is time to end at last, and I shall close with this chapter, entitled, "Of the Gift of Palatable Wisdom."

"The seventh divine gift is that of palatable wisdom. It is admitted on the summit of introversion, and crosses intelligence and

will according to their introversion in the
absolute. This relish is without end and
without measure, and flows inwardly
toward the outside, and imbibes the body
and the soul (in proportion to their re-
spective aptitude to receive it), as far as the
most intimate sense, that is to say as far as
a bodily sensation. The other senses, like
sight and hearing, take their pleasures outside in the marvels that God has created by
His glory and for the needs of man. This
incomprehensible relish, above spirit, and in
the amplitude of the soul, is without measure, and this is the Holy Spirit, the incomprehensible love of God. Below the
spirit, sensation is measured. But as the
forces are imminent, they inundate everything. Now, the Father of eternity has
adorned the introversed spirit, with enjoyment in the unity, and with active and passive comprehension in the loss of one's self,
and this spirit becomes thus the throne and

the repose of God; and the Son, eternal truth, has adorned with His own splendour introversed intelligence, in order to contemplate the aspect of enjoyment. And now the Holy Spirit would adorn the introversed will, and the immanent unity of power, so that the soul tastes, knows, and proves how great God is. This relish is so immense that the soul imagines that heaven, earth, and all that is in them should be dissolved and destroyed in this limitless taste. These delights are above and below, within and without, and have wholly enveloped and saturated the kingdom of the soul.

"Then intelligence regards simplicity from whence flow all these delights. From there the attention of illumined reason is born. It knows well, however, that it is powerless to understand these inconceivable delights, for it observes by means of a created light, while this joy is without measure. That is why reason fails in its attention; but the intelligence which is transformed by this limitless splendour contemplates without interruption the incomprehensible joy of beatitude."

It remains for me to say a word about the diverse translations of Ruysbroeck's work. Twenty years ago, Ernest Hello published a very brief volume in which are gathered, under mostly arbitrary heads, varied passages from our author, translated from a Latin translation, written in the sixteenth century by a Carthusian of Cologne, Laurentius Surius.

This translation by Surius, of a subtle and beautiful Latin, reveals scrupulously and admirably the sense of the original; but restless, lengthened, and weakened, it is like some distant picture, through impure glass, when one sees the queer colours of the primitive Flemish. There, where the author uses one word, he habitually puts in two or three

and then not content, he very often paraphrases what he has already sufficiently
translated. The anchorite has some cries
of love so intense that they are almost blas-
phemous; Surius is afraid of them, and he
says other things. At moments the old
hermit regards still outwardly, and looks, so
as to speak of God, for images in the
garden, the kitchen and in the stars; Surius
does not always dare to follow him there,
and forces himself to weaken the text or
flatters himself that he ennobles it.

"He escapes me as a vagabond"

says one of the Flemish Béguines, speaking
of Jesus, and others add:

"I keep house with Jesus.
He is mine and I am His.
He dispenses to me night and day,
He has stolen my heart;
I am engulfed in His mouth.
I have nought to do outside."

On Emerson and Other Essays

Elsewhere God says to man:

"I wish to be thy nourishment,
Thy host and thy cook.
My flesh is well prepared
On the Cross through pity for thee;
We shall eat and drink together."

The translator is frightened and transforms these singular outbursts into pale in-
terpretations. The wild and naïve aspect,
and the immense and cruel love of the
original work disappear most often in a
wise, correct, fulsome, and monotonous
claustral phraseology; though the inner
fidelity remains always irreproachable.
There are some fragments of this translation that Ernest Hello has translated in his
turn; or rather, he has assembled in arbitrary chapters, some phrases taken from diverse portions of the work and distorted
them by a double translation, and from it he

has composed a kind of cento, almost always admirable, but where, in spite of my researches, I have found only three or four bits honestly reproduced.

As for the present translation, it has no other merit than its scrupulous literalness. Perhaps, it would have been possible to render it, if not more elegant, at least more readable, and to clarify the work a little from the point of view of its theological and metaphysical phraseology. But it has seemed to me less dangerous and more loyal to hold myself to an almost blind word for word translation. I have also resisted those inevitable temptations of false splendours, for incessantly the spirit of the old monk touches strange beauties, which his discretion does not worry, and all his paths are peopled with splendid, quiet dreams, whose sleep his humility has not dared to disturb.

THE END

**RETURN
TO➡** **CIRCULATION DEPARTMENT**
202 Main Library

LOAN PERIOD 1 **HOME USE**	2	3
4	5	6

ALL BOOKS MAY BE RECALLED AFTER 7 DAYS
1-month loans may be renewed by calling 642-3405
6-month loans may be recharged by bringing books to Circulation Desk
Renewals and recharges may be made 4 days prior to due date

DUE AS STAMPED BELOW

RET'D. JUL 3 1 1982		

UNIVERSITY OF CALIFORNIA, BERKELEY
FORM NO. DD6, 60m, 12/80   BERKELEY, CA 94720

CPSIA information can be obtained
at www.ICGtesting.com
Printed in the USA
LVHW08s2147091018
593056LV00013B/335/P